Magdalen Smith is Diocesan Director of ⟨...⟩ the Diocese of Chester. She has a backgr⟨...⟩ is interested in the dialogue between faith ⟨...⟩. A retreat leader and spiritual director, she has published *Steel Angels: The personal qualities of a priest* and *Fragile Mystics: Reclaiming a prayerful life*.

UNEARTHLY BEAUTY

Through Advent with the saints

Magdalen Smith

First published in Great Britain in 2017

Society for Promoting Christian Knowledge
36 Causton Street
London SW1P 4ST
www.spck.org.uk

The author and publisher have made every effort to ensure that the external website and
email addresses included in this book are correct and up to date at the time of going to
press. The author and publisher are not responsible for the content, quality or continuing
accessibility of the sites.

Scripture quotations are taken from the New Revised Standard Version of the Bible,
Anglicized Edition, copyright © 1989, 1995 by the Division of Christian Education of the
National Council of the Churches of Christ in the USA. Used by permission. All rights
reserved.

British Library Cataloguing-in-Publication Data
A catalogue record for this book is available from the British Library

ISBN 978–0–281–07718–2
eBook ISBN 978–0–281–07719–9

Typeset by Fakenham Prepress Solutions, Fakenham, Norfolk NR21 8NN
First printed in Great Britain by Ashford Colour Press
Subsequently digitally reprinted in Great Britain

eBook by Fakenham Prepress Solutions, Fakenham, Norfolk NR21 8NN

Produced on paper from sustainable forests

To Eve Rosalind and Aidan Martin John,
my beautiful, talented, funny and flawed children
who show me God every day.
May they carry past loved ones into a glorious future

Contents

Contents

Introduction

Radical response

Arrivals are often mixed blessings, as the playwright Alan Bennett discovered when he allowed a certain Miss Shepherd to park her dilapidated van on his drive. She stayed for 15 years. Ex-nun and bag-lady, Miss Shepherd was dirty, eccentric, obstreperous and mostly ungrateful for the gentle kindness she received from Bennett over the years. The 2015 film *The Lady in the Van* comically portrays the relationship she had with him and the other inhabitants of Gloucester Crescent, the street she made her home between 1974 and 1989. Bennett, reflecting on the film (which is his own play written in 1999) on Radio 4, said with heartfelt honesty, 'Having her there taught me that I wasn't as kind hearted as I thought I might be. She was poor, she was smelly, she was difficult – but there's a place for people like that – but less so now than there was. You have to take care of people.' Miss Shepherd was no saint and probably neither is Alan Bennett, but her presence drew out of this writer what became far more than a functional response. Despite her being a genuinely difficult person, through the offering of long-term hospitality and the keeping of a watchful eye Bennett's compassionate pragmatism expanded his humanity; he became a bigger person.

Advent is about arrival too – the arrival of Jesus into our world in poverty and vulnerability amid unusual circumstances. For the world then, as now, this arrival generated a mixed response from a variety of people – anxiety, threat, expectation and hope. As Christians today we too are asked for a renewed response each year. And in our age of frenetic busyness we anticipate Christmas with a similar mixed sentiment, our hearts often sinking as we realize the shops have got there before us, often already glibly decorated by the end of October or early November as we struggle to catch up, anxious that we will not be ready for Christmas and all that it demands materially and emotionally. For people of faith, the expectant and fasting season of Advent has the capacity to diminish as we swig mulled wine and attend 'Christmas' parties from early December. We live at a time where church seasons of fasting and feasting seem much less distinctive than they once were, as much less is made of the significance and sharp-edged characteristics of this Advent time.

Within our own lives we remember those people who have been significant for us in the past. At the end of November, the Church celebrates All Saints and All Souls. All Souls in particular is making a comeback – a renewed church service that people 'get' – it feeling increasingly important for many to remember loved ones, incorporated into the 'communion of saints', who have died in the past year and beyond. In my own parish we organize this ecumenically, an opportunity to join with other communities of faith in their care for the bereaved. People find it increasingly comforting to believe that those individuals who have been important to them somehow remain inextricably bound up with the community of God's eternal people, a connection which breaks through death making the transition from this life to a heavenly one. We all need others who have loved and inspired us and we are always partly formed by those who continually challenge us to grow into more expansive people. Such individuals might have inspired us to be better people, might have demonstrated a faithfulness to us; ordinary yet extraordinary, they are also people who might have just landed up in our lives, like Miss Shepherd.

As Christian people living in an 'age of anxiety' we must challenge ourselves to live distinctively, to think carefully about how we might 'keep the faith'. To do this, we can draw not only on people known to us but on those who form part of our faith heritage. This book provides a fresh journey through Advent, inspired by the well-known as well as the more obscure holy people from the past, those whom the Church calls 'saints'. As we read and ponder we might also bear in mind those individuals who have shaped and changed us, those whom we have known personally (perhaps still know now), those who are set firmly in our lives as 'family' as well as those who arrive in our lives in random and unintentional ways. This book is an attempt to bring to light some of those perhaps forgotten individuals in the history of our faith as well as in the biblical tradition, to see what wisdom and inspiration they can bring to this season to make it crisper and more incisive. Its reflections offer refreshed perspectives on traditional Advent themes such as expectation, fulfilment, hospitality and hope, which seek to connect with our own lives lived as contemporary people of faith.

Like Miss Shepherd, saints ironically do not always feel very saintly – they are weird and colourful people, often driven and visionary, living strange and unconventional lives. Watchers of *The Lady in the Van* discover, as the film unfolds, that after a previous life in a convent Miss Shepherd is actually on the run, having accidentally killed someone. Saints are people who strive in a single-minded vision to follow God, sometimes atoning for a previous dispassionate or selfish life. More often than not they live distinctively, sometimes unusually, and by doing so grab our attention. We love people who are different as well as people who are brave, who have the courage to 'keep the faith' in whatever way: individuals who live intentionally with our faith's distinguishing marks upon them as they rail against living in a monochrome and often cruel world. Often their brokenness through divine transformation inspires us, their eccentric habits enable us to look on our own lifestyles with new vision, their sacrifice challenges us to be more compassionate people. Turning away from the signs of the times, going against the flow, they grasp a more powerful kingdom vision. Embedded in their lives is a mysterious dynamic happening that, however strange, kindles in us a renewed response to the world, enabling us to move closer to holiness, to be more filled with love ourselves. These are people like Miss Shepherd, who for all their quirky quaintness and 'vagabond nobility' inspire us to be far less ordinary than we often allow our lives to become. They are people of unearthly beauty who show us a deeper understanding of the fluid nature of divine grace.

We cannot begin to think about Christmas without Mary, who becomes one of the archetypical Advent saints we traditionally remember on the fourth Sunday of Advent. Without her there would be no Incarnation, no nativity, no eternal message of joy for a pained and weary world. I own a print by the artist and priest Nigel Done. The painting, called *Overflowing Moments*, is of Mary herself, stepping into what we hope is a warm bath. It is a beautiful picture of an everyday moment in a humble home. Above her naked form the supersonic figure of Gabriel hovers, his presence illuminating the whole picture. Arms outstretched, Mary looks up, taken aback at this sudden and astonishing presence, wondering about its significance. Her story too is a contemporary one – an ordinary yet extraordinary woman whose decision to say 'yes' to God meant a definitive perspective of hope, keenly offered into a dark world that would eventually murder her son. Young and poor, she carries a gravitas and resilience way beyond her years and social status.

Europe still reels from the ISIL attacks on three cultural venues in the city of Paris, as well as from the terrorist attack on Bastille Day 2016, when a truck drove into a crowd of tourists gathered on the Promenade des Anglais in Nice. At the Bataclan Theatre in Paris, 89 ordinary Parisians and many others lost their lives in an atrocious terrorist attack on 13 November 2015, including Hélène Leiris, whose husband Antoine posted a moving statement and tribute to his wife a few days later. His extraordinary statement of intentional 'non-hatred' has been an inspirational message for millions who have viewed it. Through the killing of Hélène, Antoine was left alone with his 17-month-old son. An ordinary family made famous by global events. An ordinary man made extraordinary by his response to the malevolent events of those who perpetrated the violence. His response holds a mysterious holiness which is Mary's story too – a woman unknown yet catapulted to fame through the unusual events which happened to her. Hers too was to be a story double-edged and tragic in her own ability to carry the pain of untimely cruelty and premeditated death. Hers is an example of how, through a belief in the ultimate victory of hope and concerted love, the power of faith can dissolve and unmask all that is evil and violent in the world. Her advent is the choice of saying 'yes' to all that is good, however unbelievable the possibility of the world changing and whatever the cost. Saints are made every day and from humble beginnings.

But this is not sugary sentiment. We are living through an era in the world's history where fundamentalism is rearing an exceptionally ugly head, when an understanding of God as a purist, literalist tyrant is one which is as real as the 200 people who died in Paris in November 2015. As Christians and just as decent human beings we have a choice, as Antoine Leiris did, to turn away from such a perspective and to see the beauty and possibility within humanity as well as the immense power that un-hatred yields. It is an outlook such as this that will help us stand out as Christians today. But we cannot do it alone. We need the renewed inspiration of God as well as of the holy people of both past and present who made and make such choices too.

Advent sweeps in like a sudden bitter wind, taking our breath away with its icy freshness, challenging us to rethink this season, nudging us to relive it with renewed imagination. Advent is opportunity for us to prepare for the momentous events of the Incarnation, the extraordinary happening of God becoming man, the fact not of the abandonment of the earth but the adventure of a God who lives and loves among his people always.

ADVENT SAINTS

Andrew
A life less ordinary

Andrew sounds like the name of the bloke next door. Your really rather average man who works in IT, has a wife who works nine to five as a doctor's receptionist, has two children and a dog and goes to Spain on holiday (and apologies if I'm offending anyone, but bear with me). We probably all know friends, neighbours, uncles or taxi drivers called Andrew – it's an ordinary name for an ordinary man. Andrew as a fisherman on Galilee symbolizes just such a person. The apostle Andrew's festival is on 30 November and, depending on when Advent falls, is sometimes included at the beginning of the season. He is included here because his life has some important things to say as most of us arrive with a slight sense of resignation, maybe boredom or even panic, at the beginning of December, knowing that as Christians, amid all the material mania, we are asked to mark this season well.

Truth is, the Bible doesn't tell us that much about him. He was one of the first four disciples called by Jesus and in the Synoptic Gospels is described as a fisherman who worked alongside his brother Simon Peter as well as the brothers James and John. John's Gospel has it that all four were disciples of John the Baptist – perhaps a hint that spiritual discipline was woven into their already physically demanding lives. Andrew also has the reputation of being the first missionary – he is the one who introduces Peter to Jesus and he is also the disciple who accompanies Jesus right up to the end of his life. So maybe Jesus' apparently blasé and spontaneous call to come and join him was much more premeditated than we give him credit for. For here was a man who understood physical discipline and faithfulness as well as hardship. Andrew is reputed to have travelled on several missionary journeys in Scythia, and to have finally been martyred on an X-shaped cross because he believed himself not worthy of being killed on the same kind of cross as Jesus. He became the patron saint of Scotland because it is reputed that his relics were brought there in the eighth century.

It would be easy to romanticize Andrew's call to discipleship – bright boats heavy with slippery fish, waves sparkling with spray amid the camaraderie of a busy industry. But most likely, a first-century fisherman's life brought distinct hardships, with competition among boats and heavy and dangerous work, heaving nets which cut the flesh, battling with unpredictable weather. So here the call feels smooth, easy; Jesus says, 'Follow me', and Andrew drops everything. Dietrich Bonhoeffer, in a reflection on the call of the fishermen, talks of 'a ruthless silence' in the text in terms of any explanation as to why these rough brothers chose to follow Jesus so immediately.[1] But it is a mistake, he says, for us to psychologize about their reasoning and if we do then we miss the point. Miss the point because the call is about Jesus who is God – it is God who calls and invites a response.

There has in recent years been a resurgence in the idea of the presence of God woven into ordinary life. At the heart of Advent and Christmas is the intertwining of both the ordinary and the extraordinary – God coming into the world through the miraculous arrival of a baby – a stupendous yet earthed event which happens every day around the globe. Advent includes several ordinary people, like Andrew the fisherman, who respond fairly swiftly to God's 'big asks' – Mary, Joseph and Elizabeth, transforming their own lives into ones which contribute and dissolve into something much more significant. It can be argued, therefore, that for people who *are* ordinary, who have not much to lose, for people who are not obsessed with who they are or what they have in terms of money or status, it is much, much easier to leave even this ordinariness behind to follow a vision which is expansive and life-changing. Andrew carries within him the quality of *single-mindedness* – of retaining an ability to see the power in the person of Jesus himself and the significance this has for human life. Within the call of Andrew is the archetypical 'call and response' – a pure and unadulterated obedience to the challenge to understand God as God and to enter into an adventure which is simultaneously new and unmarked, and woven into the naturalness of the journey of life itself. For fishermen, those who lived with the beauty as well as the terror of the sea, perhaps such knowledge was inherent.

I am currently accompanying someone who is exploring the possibility of being ordained in the Anglican Church as a priest and leader. His name is Andrew too but he likes to be called Drew. Drew works currently in an ordinary job – as a distribution manager for the ordinary and well-known supermarket Asda. Drew is simply a pleasant and ordinary bloke – and yet he is much more than this. Pass him in the street and you might not assume he is deeply devoted to Jesus. Sit opposite him on your way to work and you might not realize that he is doing something brave and obedient by helping to initiate a new church on a bleak housing estate in his parish. Drew reminds me of the disciple Andrew: a decent and resolute man who understands where his allegiance lies because he is continually able to put his ordinariness, his individuality, his own agenda to one side to play his part in participating in God's kingdom.

Bonhoeffer observes that not one word of praise is given to the disciple for his decision to follow Jesus. This is not something worthy or something to do with *him* – 'We are not expected to contemplate the disciple, but only him who calls, and his absolute authority. According to our text there is no road to faith or discipleship, no other road – only obedience to the call of Jesus.'[2] The call to vocation, that of following Christ, is always something of an echo: the call from outside of ourselves, as happened here with Andrew and his brother. But with this, the recognition that this was somehow a waited-for, expected resonance of something deep within. The meeting here took place between Jesus hollering over the waves to Andrew and Andrew's immediate response, perhaps the culmination of years of the inner workings of God praying within him, a man who, like the sea he sailed upon, had hidden depths.

A recent initiative by SPCK and others – Prayers on the Move – aims at tapping into the spirituality inherent in many people. A recent survey of 2,000 people states that 42 per cent of adults admit that they pray. Prayer is a reaching out, beyond ourselves or delving deep within, an activity that many people do without even realizing it, as Richard Chartres, the recently retired Bishop of London, explains. In the early part of 2016 thousands of prayer posters were placed on public transport in both London and Newcastle as part of a wider initiative, with the hope that 'reading a simple prayer in the anonymity of the Tube or the bus will give people an opportunity to listen to the Spirit's inner voice'.[3] Interestingly, it is often when we have time, when we are waiting on station platforms or in bus shelters, that we give our minds and hearts a little more opportunity for our souls to connect with that which is 'other'. This is a clever and creative initiative and connects with our subject here. As Chartres says, 'Jesus met ordinary people where they were, and provoked them to think about things eternal.'[4]

The call to follow Christ usually involves bravery, as does fishing. Jesus knew what this call would involve, which is why he chose this profession as he gathered his closest inner circle. Wrapped up in this bravery is the fact that there is no necessary blueprint for discipleship. We walk our own path with God, and while we can walk in others' footsteps and can be inspired by giant faith-lives, our own path remains uniquely our own. To follow Jesus gives us no easily understandable lifestyle or clear-sighted goal to strive after. It is a much less glamorous and identifiable call – to follow the actual person who is Christ, 'It is a gracious call, a gracious commandment. It transcends the difference between the law and the gospel. Christ calls, the disciple follows; that is grace and commandment in one.'[5]

So much about Advent is not only about waiting – waiting for Jesus to arrive – but about journeying. Many of the saints had travel at the heart of their lives and ministries, and many of the Advent stories have the subject of journeying at their centre. This most mesmeric of church seasons provides the meeting of our inner awareness of God, who asks us to step out of the boat or get on to the bus, connecting us with a more expansive and life-giving vision which will take us we know not where.

Prayer ideas

- Pray for fishermen, especially those who work in particularly dangerous conditions.
- Pray for those finding it hard to respond to God's call.
- Pray to discern and feel God's presence in the ordinary aspects of your life.
- Pray for those who work in the transport industry.
- Visit <www.prayeronthemove.com> for more ideas and resources.

Charles de Foucauld
With and not for

The word 'little' is at the heart of the Christmas story. We sing about the 'little' town of Bethlehem, often concentrating our thoughts around the fact that God came into the world as a 'little child', both vulnerable and awesome like every baby that is born on the planet, whoever he or she may be. It is worth pondering on this word, for 'little' ironically speaks volumes. It reminds us that God chose to come to be with us, not as the mighty and all-conquering Messiah that the Jews were expecting but in an unobtrusive and very 'normal' way. Jesus is born alongside ordinary life being lived. With this we are asked to take down the God we often place on a pedestal of importance – the pedestal that seeks to make him the omnipotent Somebody we look up to, who controls our lives and micromanages the universe. But this God, like so many statues, is cast in cold and sober stone.

In December, we remember the life of Charles de Foucauld, the aristocrat-cum-hermit who founded simple fraternities of men and women living *with* and not *for* the poor and continuing to do so in small, often invisible groups in some of the toughest and most uninviting environments around the globe. These 'communities' (and even this seems too grand a word) are known as the Little Brothers and the Little Sisters of Jesus.

Charles was born into a devout and wealthy family in Strasbourg in 1858. Both his parents died before he was six and he was brought up by his grandfather, who pandered to his every desire, perhaps to make up for the inevitable grief both felt. During his young life, Charles undertook his military service, lost his faith and squandered a fortune. Not knowing where his life was leading he disguised himself as a holy man and travelled to Morocco, where he found his faith trickling back, partly through his encounter with a wise and discerning priest, Abbé Huvelin. After a simple confessional-type conversion, Charles was overcome by a genuine experience of Jesus and he became a Trappist monk.

But Charles's dream was to found his own order and one which had some ascetic rigour to it. To test this out, he lived for two further years as a simple domestic servant to a community of Poor Clares in Nazareth itself. It was here that he formulated his spiritual ethic that 'Nazareth is everywhere', feeling passionately that his call was to live out a simple life of work alongside ordinary people under a personal discipline of prayer and essential living. Charles progressed to Béni Abbès in Algeria, finally settling in Tamanghasset in the Sahara, 400 miles from any large centre. Here he built himself a long, narrow hermitage with an altar at one end and an ever-open door. He lived among the Tuareg people, compiling the first Tuareg grammar and dictionary, also translating the Gospels into this language. Over time he helped many of the native people to replace their precarious reed dwellings with sturdier clay, constructing whole towns, even a fort to protect the surrounding population against invading Turkish troops, then allies of the Germans. Charles met his death in 1916 when, through a tragic misunderstanding, he was shot dead by an anti-French tribesman. He was beatified by Pope Benedict XVI in 2005.

Charles's spirituality had at its heart the idea of living naturally and prayerfully alongside the Tuareg people, in whose natural environment he was a guest. His was not a drive to convert through heavy proselytizing but his 'rule' was an offering of silence, love and practical help as a living example of the gospel. Even now the ethos of the Little Brothers is to live in 'little', family-type communities who

> unobtrusively keep a routine of communal prayer and silent adoration, but every day they go out in their working clothes to do the same sort of job that their neighbours are doing and to offer them an unstinted friendship in the doing of it. Out of sight, out of mind of the Church as a whole, way below the poverty line, scattered in their twos and threes across the face of the earth, they do not work for their neighbours, they work with them. Their role is that of prayer and of a silent, hidden presence of love.[1]

There is a conscious decision for those brothers and sisters not even to reveal their own skills or education – their intention is to recreate the life of Jesus lived in Nazareth in the early days of his mostly unrevealed life, in an attitude of self-effacement.

Charles de Foucauld helps us to return to the simple essence that is the Christ-mass event. This event, like the presents we open on

Christmas Day, has for the most part become far too glamorous and elaborate. We 'wrap' it up with so much, and as Christian people we are challenged to fight through the externals to the little yet powerful centre of its message, which is Jesus being born in an unknown stable, God coming to live alongside his people. Charles's deliberate poverty seemed to grow the more he gave up as well as the greater the solitude he experienced: 'I relish the charms of solitude more and more, and I am trying to find out how to enter into a deeper and deeper solitude.'[2] Such negation of material things, together with aloneness, is a challenging concept for us to think about during Advent, a season often overcome with unnecessary 'stuff' and peopled with sociability. Charles's was a singular vision of a simple and 'little' life which enabled him to see God in a uni-focused way, 'More than fifteen hours with nothing else to do but gaze on you, Lord, and tell you that I love you.'[3] He knelt, often completely still, lost in contemplation, his eyes fixed on the altar he had made and the host within the tabernacle upon it, usually for seven hours on weekdays and nearly all day on Sundays and feast days. He believed that the great love he felt for the people he lived among, a love which grew over the years, stemmed from this deep love for God. Over the years he wrote hundreds of simple meditations which were meant for the eyes of no one but himself, exemplifying the idea that, as a Little Brother of Jesus, he was to resist any attempt at fame or renown.

Charles de Foucauld is a prophetic and powerful example of how we also approach 'the other', whoever that may be. As a Director of Ordinands I have on one of my candidates' questionnaires, 'Would you or would you not take part in a multi-faith service?' Of course, people offer a multitude of thought-provoking, often sensitive answers to this question and there has to be freedom to do so. I myself trained ecumenically and in a multicultural and multi-faith city, so have several friends who are of a different denomination from my own. At Christmas time many involved in leadership often participate in ecumenical Christmas services as we do in my own parish, holding an outdoor carol service in the pedestrian area of the town. An article from the Hermitary website says this: 'Charles de Foucauld is a complex historical figure within Catholicism, history and eremitism. That is to say, he is uniquely modern, and his life was an unconscious striving to attain an ecumenical eremitism, a universal eremitism.'[4]

With what those outside the Church experience as 'in-house' fighting, we are called to grow not only a love and acceptance of our Christian brothers and sisters of other denominations but to tread carefully when we enter the domain of those of a completely different faith. So much of this is about a standing back rather than a ploughing in, developing a genuine desire to understand the basic theologies and practices of other belief systems. The issue of the developing of friendship coming before any religious debate feels particularly acute for us in an age of religious extremism. The recent national move of British Muslims to hold the equivalent of a mosque 'open day' to begin to dispel attitudes of prejudice and ignorance was a brave step in the right direction.

Some might accuse Charles, as well as ourselves, of naivety when we insist on a 'with rather than for' attitude to service and evangelism. Yet so much genuine, helpful and realistic spiritual care comes to fruition just like this. An episode of the TV comedy *Rev* shows Adam Smallbone, the Anglican vicar, attempting to make links with his local mosque in order to work together for the good of the community in the rejuvenation of a children's playground. The contrast between the successful Imam Yussef and the failing and continuously blundering Adam is as apparent from the size of their respective congregations as from the money they make for the joint project. Adam, although a comic figure, is portrayed as 'little' – his leadership vulnerable, lonely yet still dignified. But genuine friendship is cemented between the two faith centres and a new respect formed through this joint venture.[5]

Charles de Foucauld believed that the Holy Spirit functioned as the drawing together of individual people. His was not the self-conscious attempt at ecumenical or multi-faith 'dialogue' in the traditional sense but rather a searching for the presence and spirit of Jesus Christ within what existed already in the beauty and strength of an established religious tradition. He advocated the practice of *listening* as an evangelistic tool, that before any gospel can be proclaimed, the evangelist must understand and respect the world view of the other. Here is a deep sense of 'Christian presence', the living out of a small yet deeply authentic faith, incarnated and echoed in the birth of God as a tiny baby who comes always to live not *for* but *with* all of humanity.

Prayer ideas

- Pray for Christian churches and leaders of other denominations in the place where you live.
- Pray for an end to all religious extremism and for a new tolerance and spirit of friendship and understanding to grow nationally and internationally.
- Pray for those who live out their Christian calling alone.
- Pray for Christians working in cultures distinctively different from their own.

Francis Xavier
Pioneer of the East

In my early 20s, I spent a year in South Africa with the Anglican mission organization United Society Partners in the Gospel (USPG). Nowadays, the word 'missionary' has fallen into a slightly unpolitically correct pool of unsound words. We talk instead of those in 'the mission field'. But the year I spent with this organization was a hugely formative one for me, for USPG was, and is, a visionary and enlightened establishment. My year was part of the Society's Encounter and Exchange programme – the idea that young people would go and volunteer in a church community abroad, completely absorb themselves in the experience and then return to share something of what they had learned with their own church community at home. It was a brilliant concept and one which also set me on a decisive journey towards ordination.

Prior to departure I participated with other young people in three weeks of 'cross-cultural training', heightening my awareness of all the cultural assumptions and prejudices I carried as a white, Western female in the early 1990s. My year was spent having such prejudices shattered as I realized, through talking and living among the 'rainbow people of God', that South Africa was, ironically, far from 'black and white' in its attitude to the diversity of humanity living there as well as to apartheid itself. As part of the experience I lived in a township with a white Afrikaans priest and his family for a month, spent time helping at a rural retreat centre in the KwaZulu area and hitchhiked around the country with some friends, listening to the stories of ordinary people.

These days those who choose to work in the Christian 'mission field' go already skilled as teachers or engineers and occasionally just as clergy. But overall the attitude is very much a respectful one which approaches a new situation with 'What will we learn?' rather than 'What can we take?' Most people with any knowledge of the Anglican Communion will understand that Christianity is growing rapidly and persistently in the Global South, and consequently those of us who struggle to fill our churches need to look and listen hard to why this is so and what is going on.

But this was not always the case in the world. On 3 December the Church remembers the legacy of Francis Xavier, one of the co-founders of the Society of Jesus and the man who proselytized the most in all of Asia in his time. Born in 1503, Francis was from the kingdom of Navarre, in the Basque country. A Roman Catholic, his was a purposeful mission to bring the good news of the gospel of Jesus to those who had simply not heard it: 'Many, many people hereabouts are not becoming Christians for one reason only: there is nobody to make them Christians.'[1]

Francis led an extensive mission in Asia and was the first missionary to venture into Borneo, the Maluku Islands and eventually Japan. He is considered to be one of the greatest missionaries since St Paul, reputed to have converted around 30,000 people to the faith. He concentrated mostly on countries within the Portuguese Empire of the time and built 40 churches along the coast of southern India and Sri Lanka, then Ceylon. In 1549 Francis met a man called Anjiro who was fleeing for his life, accused of murder. Anjiro became the first Japanese Christian and eased Francis's entry into his country.

In terms of conversion, Francis's success was inevitably mixed. In Japan, where many were already Buddhist or Shinto, he found that Christianity brought contrasting and problematic beliefs. Those who were recipients of his message struggled with the idea of how a 'good' God could also be responsible for evil, and both religions struggled with the idea that their ancestors might be in 'hell'. But for 45 years the Jesuits were the only missionaries in Asia. Francis eventually died of a fever on the Chinese island of Shangchuan in 1552. During his lifetime Francis was invited to be the head of St Paul's College in Goa, a pioneer seminary for the education of secular priests. This became the Jesuit headquarters in Asia, and Goa remains a central pilgrimage place, where Francis's relics are kept in an ornate silver casket which depicts 32 episodes from his life.

As with many missionaries of his time, Francis's reputation and methods for conversion have been criticized, but he has also been praised for his progressive attitude: for instance, his insistence that missionaries took local customs seriously and made every effort to learn the local language of the indigenous people with whom they chose to live and work. His reputation becomes shadier, as there were rumours he was involved in the surreptitious cruelty of the Goan Inquisition and its establishment, perpetuated for nearly 250 years, which was established to punish apostate new Christians and Muslims who had converted to Catholicism, as well as their descendants who were accused of continuing their original religious practices in private. However, Francis died before this Inquisition really became paramount in the region so perhaps it is unlikely he played a large part within it.

The term 'pioneer' priest has taken on new meaning in recent years. The Anglican Church has recognized it needs to reimagine what being a missional church might look like in the context of twenty-first-century Britain. To be a specifically 'pioneer' minister is to have a proven track record of initiating 'church' from scratch – Francis Xavier would have felt right at home! We need continuously to reflect on what a right approach to spreading the gospel should be in whatever land and 'culture' we find ourselves. Our materialistic and often weary Western society is one that is always hungry to hear good news which brings hope and life – hungry because business and pressure and 'stuff' don't ultimately satisfy. We already live in a context which might be considered a 'mission field'.

The Taiwanese theologian Choan-Seng Song suggests that there should be an awareness and gradual moving towards the light which is Christ, but a Christ who ultimately transcends all cultures to bring a human and divine freedom.

> The light burns. It gives warmth. It gives hope. And as the dreamer timidly advances toward the light, he discovers that there are many others moving toward it from different directions – from behind iron curtains, from across human barriers, from behind the walls of our frightened souls. Yes, we all need that light, for that light is the only hope – we, the poor and rich, the oppressed and the oppressors, the theists and the atheists, Christians, Muslims, Jews, Buddhists and Hindus. We must all get to that light, for it is the light of love and life, the light of hope and the future . . . And so God moves on, God moves in Europe, in Africa, in the Americas, in Asia. Until the time when the communion of love is firmly established in the world of strife and conflict, of pain and suffering, God moves on in compassion.[2]

People need to hear God's good news – the story of Jesus Christ, living, dying, rising for the sake of the love of the world, providing an alternative to hatred and suspicion and the violence which results from both of those. As followers we venture into unknown territory every day, where we live, where we work, even perhaps among our own family. Christmas time is also a classic opportunity for our churches to reach out to those who are unused to the message we already know well. Like Francis, we are called to spread the good news of a loving and forgiving God to whoever is willing to listen and care, perhaps especially during a season when people feel a simultaneous sense of pressure as well as reflection.

For Francis this began by sowing the seeds of friendship, as he believed that the better friends you were with another person the easier it became in terms of being straightforward about the gospel and the things that mattered. It is of paramount importance too that those of us intent on evangelizing remember that Christ's presence is embodied in those who need God's love the most. He is present in those who are hurting, hungry, poor and lost. Nadia Bolz-Weber, in her book *Accidental Saints*, shares a timely reminder which underpins all proactive Christian evangelism:

> And to be clear, Christ does not come to us *as* the poor and hungry. Because, as anyone for whom the poor are not an abstraction but actual flesh-and-blood people knows, the poor and hungry and imprisoned are not a romantic special class of Christ-like people. And those who meet their needs are not a romantic special class of Christ-like people. We are equally as sinful and saintly as the other. No, Christ comes to us in the *needs* of the poor and hungry, needs that are met by another so that the gleaming redemption of God might be known . . . the fact is, we are all, at once, bearers of the gospel as well as receivers of it.[3]

Prayer ideas

- Pray for those serving in the 'mission field' in countries and cultures different from their own.
- Pray for those who are persecuted for their faith.
- Pray for pioneer ordinands, priests and their families.
- Pray for an openness to other Christians from around the world.

John of Damascus
Matter matters

Kissing. People feel so differently about it. I've been in one church where an all-out debate developed during a PCC meeting around what the protocol should be during the Peace. Should we shake hands, give bear hugs or simply stay in our seats (much safer)? When guests arrive at your house or when you meet a friend in the street, how do you respond? Is he or she a 'hug' kind of person, or more of a kiss on one cheek, or two – maybe even three? These days who do you kiss? For me, it's my husband, my children still, friends and family and often even the cat, of which I am extremely fond.

Kissing has perhaps always been somewhat controversial – a simultaneously private and public expression of love, sometimes passion. But it can often also be a sign of respect or courtesy for those we know and like, as well as a genuine expression of welcome. And this is the crux of the matter. We tend to kiss people and not things. As human beings most of us need and enjoy demonstrating some kind of tangible expression of love towards others, whoever they might be. But we don't often do this with objects, unless it's a cuddly toy.

In the eighth and ninth centuries in the Christian world of the Middle East a controversy raged. A monk and priest known as John of Damascus was at its forefront. Born into a wealthy Arab–Christian family, John is believed to have held a significant position (as his father had previously done) as the chief administrator to the Muslim Caliph of Damascus during his early life. Around 725 John resigned this office and became a monk at the monastery of Mar Saba near Bethlehem. It is here that his lasting legacy began to unfold, and it began when Emperor Leo III outlawed the veneration of icons.

The conflict had been around under the surface of the religious life of the region for years. At a time when Islam, a religion that refused absolutely to depict any images of God, was spreading throughout the Mediterranean, it was perhaps inevitable that some of its principles challenged Christianity to ask questions of itself. Culturally, it was perfectly acceptable to show respect for the Creator by bowing and kissing icons, but the controversy centred around the second of the Ten Commandments:

> You shall not make for yourself an idol, whether in the form of anything that is in heaven above, or that is on the earth beneath, or that is in the water under the earth. You shall not bow down to them or worship them.

Aided by the explosive eruption of a local volcano which created havoc and danger for the local population and the tidal wave which followed, Leo, listening to the musing of his bishops, concluded that God himself was angry and that things must change.

In 730 the emperor commanded the destruction of all religious depictions of the divine, be they icons, mosaics, paintings or statues. The age of the iconoclasts ('image smashers') had tragic consequences, as a huge amount of ancient and exquisite art was destroyed. From his place of seclusion and silence John spoke out. He argued that no physical depiction of Christ should be *worshipped*; rather, it should be *venerated*. The distinction is crucial. Worship suggests potentially unquestioning or uncritical love, in this case a love of an object as opposed to the subject matter. Veneration suggests that the object is simply regarded with respect and reverence. A quote from one of the saint's treatises puts it like this:

> I do not worship matter, I worship the God of matter, who became matter for my sake and deigned to inhabit matter, who worked out my salvation through matter. I will not cease from honouring that matter which works for my salvation. I venerate it, though not as God.[1]

John's argument was that the depiction of images simply enables believers to focus and remember Christ's sacrifice and salvation. Images such as icons are to be understood as aids to prayer rather than idolatrous objects of worship themselves. John drew on the writings of the early Church Fathers such as Basil the Great, who emphasized this understanding – that an object such as an icon provides simply the gateway to the divine, a point of departure for those who are seeking an experience of God in worship. Underpinning it all was John's deep recognition of an incarnate God as One who came into the world in human form and flesh, a point in human history where heaven touched earth. He argued therefore that since the unseen God had become flesh and blood there is logically no blasphemy in painting visible representations of Jesus or the saints. Icon writers, as they are known to this day, understand the (often painstaking) painting of icons as a genuine act of worship.

After his death and after years of further dissatisfaction and bloodshed over these issues, John's writings played an important role during the Second Ecumenical Council of Nicea in 787, which convened to settle once and for all the controversy over the icon dispute. Overall, John contributed to the history and theology of the Church by writing three major treatises, all of which expounded the faith and the earliest of which established his reputation, *Apologetic Treatises against those Decrying the Holy Images*. His most important theological work – *The Fount of Wisdom* – is a summary of the theology of Eastern Orthodoxy. He also wrote many hymns which are still used in Orthodox liturgical practice today.

Advent is a short season of both incarnation and idolatry. It is so easy for all of us to worship those things which are a long way from the essence and sharp reality of the Christmas story. But we are people of flesh and blood who need to be helped to understand who God is and how to experience his presence with us in our chaotic yet embodied lives. Living in a visual world enables us to formulate a theology in a different and potentially more powerful way than one which is created by words. A visual person myself, I have seen people's lives transformed through an experience of looking at particular art and images of God. My own mother, a trained iconographer, has worshipped in Orthodox churches for over 20 years and I have sometimes accompanied her. This tradition, where the congregation stand throughout worship, where an atmosphere of reverence is created through an emphasis on the sensual as incense is swung back and forth and where the walls are lined with vibrant and often unusual images of the holy people from the past, has a richness and powerful transcendence that our more Protestant forms of worship do not. There is something too about the respectful veneration of such a sanctified space and the objects within it which speaks into Advent, where often there seems no time to immerse ourselves in any sense of the sacred. Our sense of the sacramental is perhaps shifting and it is traditions such as the Orthodox that pull us back to appreciate the importance of understanding certain objects, spaces and experiences as distinctively liminal and numinous.

Studying art history at university, I too have been influenced by and continue to enjoy different images of Christ, biblical characters and theological concepts through the visual as opposed to the literal. Sacred art enriches, expands and continually challenges my understanding of who God is, and also how he interacts with the world. The resource pack *The Christ We Share* produced originally by USPG depicts images of Jesus from around the world with explanation of both artist and cultural meaning. The Incarnation means that Christ can and indeed must be understood through the eyes and life experience of the cultural context where people of the faith live and breathe and move.

With this comes the challenge to know that the Christ-event transcends all cultures and history, pushing us from creating and keeping Christ in our own image alone to appreciating a new understanding of him through the eyes of others. The working through of this continually prevents us retaining God in an image and a theological understanding which suits us. John of Damascus is a saint who challenges his readers to experience the 'God of matter, who matters' – a divinity whose hand is at work in all matter, the cross, the rock, the tomb, the altar, even the ink in which the Gospels were written. To quote John again:

> How could God be born out of material things which have no existence in themselves? God's body is God because he joined it to his person by a union which shall never pass away. Because of this I salute all matter with reverence because God has filled it with his grace and power. Through it my salvation has come to me . . . Thus either do away with the honour and veneration all these material things deserve, or accept the tradition of the Church and the veneration of icons. Learn to reverence God and his friends; follow the inspiration of the Holy Spirit. Never despise matter, for matter is not despicable. God has made nothing despicable. Rather, contemplate the glory of the Lord, for his face has been unveiled.[2]

Prayer ideas

- Pray for the Orthodox Church, giving thanks for the richness of this Christian tradition.

- Pray for all who work in the visual arts, particularly those of Christian faith.
- Pray for icon writers.
- Pray for monastic communities and their witness, especially those you know.

Nicholas Ferrar
New monastic

———◆———

Family. The word is loaded. Loaded because most of us have ambivalent feelings surrounding the people we regard as 'family'. The concept of who exactly family *is* for us is now shaped by a society more fluid and mobile, morally changed and charged than it was years ago. Today, our families are so much more complicated and complex, often feeling like a cell that morphs and clusters. I have been a part of a variety of 'families' over the years – the initial small nuclear unit of two parents and an only child, the second cousins I lived with during the final year of A levels, and the family who were part of the church where I was an intern in London. I rented a room on the top floor of their townhouse but spent many evenings enjoying their embracing, generous hospitality of endless turkey stir-frys and red wine in a warm kitchen. Over the years my own family of husband and two children has included and adopted a variety of troubled and wonderful individuals, enveloping and releasing the broken, lonely and transient, the characterful and colourful – people I would consider now to be as much 'family' as friends.

The Church debates the ethics of what and who is 'family' on a regular basis. Many of the conservative faithful argue that there is nothing more authentic or powerful than the traditional unit of Christian husband, wife and children which models a sense of healthy faith and social stability in an upturned world where the rug has been pulled from under a previously accepted ethical table. And there is much truth in that – I am proud to be a part of such a family. But even with such happiness, living within it is far from easy. Our families are the private places where those closest to us see us at our worst – tired, anxious, ugly and small-minded. They are the people who love us, as God does, regardless of all of that – those who see the dirt and dust and scars behind the varnished masks we wear once we step outside the door.

But there is also love to be found in other models of 'family', in other human commitments – in the gay couple bringing up a child who is not theirs, in the parents who are divorced who whole-heartedly embrace the children of their new partner. And then there is our so-called 'church family' – that dysfunctional, unstructured body of polished and ragged people whom we wrestle to love because they are damaged and disappointing and unkind so often. Our faith invites us to take seriously every person who is baptized, every person who considers him or herself to be part of this 'family'. And like the father of the Prodigal Son, we are called to welcome back into its folds those who, like a butterfly, settle for a time and then flit off to somewhere more fragrant, only to return mysteriously when the ministry and message is sweet and easy. Christmas time, for example.

On 4 December, the day of his death in 1637, the lectionary celebrates the life of Nicholas Ferrar, founder of the Little Gidding community. The son of a London merchant, Nicholas was both businessman and politician. Nicholas was closely connected with the Virginia Company, the group that established the American colony in 1607, but he also entered Parliament, becoming part of a court faction that challenged the financial oversight of several such colonial ventures including the East India Company. Eventually, disillusioned and facing bankruptcy, Nicholas, along with his brother John, decided on a drastic change of lifestyle. In 1626 he left London, and on the death of his father was able to purchase a manor house on a deserted estate called Little Gidding in the then county of Huntingdonshire (now Cambridgeshire). The family restored the abandoned church there and formulated a life of material simplicity and spirituality. Numbering about 30, they lived each day around a strict discipline of daily prayer. Each day, prayers were said faith-fully and methodically in the Great Chamber of the house, with daily prayers also being said in the church for Morning and Evening Prayer. Nicholas was ordained deacon by William Laud but stead-fastly refused priesthood, and the community was never a formally religious one – there was no specific 'rule' or vows that were taken. It was, rather, an ordinary family modelling a version of how the Christian life could be lived, centred around the offices within the Book of Common Prayer.

The reputation of the Ferrar household spread and over the years many visitors were attracted to the simple vision lived out by this family. King Charles I visited on several occasions, briefly taking refuge there in 1645. Nicholas was also friends with the poet George Herbert, who is reputed on his deathbed to have asked him to publish a collection of poems known as *The Temple*, a request Nicholas honoured in the same year. The Ferrars also had a ministry to the children in the locality, supporting them in health and education matters. The community was broken up in 1646 by the Puritans who, suspicious of it, feared that it might be encouraging practices from the Roman Church secretly within England's green lands. All of Nicholas's writings were destroyed.

Advent is a season which gets its fair share of family pressure. Most of us feel something of this through the beguiling unreality of Christmas advertisements, which often suggest that our Christmas Day should centre around the perfect upwardly mobile family of well-scrubbed children, harmony and a table groaning with an organic roast. Lest such a vision oppresses us we can remind ourselves of the first 'family' that gathered around the Christ child, the ragamuffin and divinely handpicked family, shepherds and wisdom seekers, beasts and overworked hoteliers. God comes to earth out of divine choice and appears in a far from idealized place: the inns were full and there had been no previous trips to Mothercare – a manger would do as cradle and 'Mary and Joseph would scarcely have won the prize for the most splendidly organized and perfectly prepared Christmas party'.[1]

Advent is, as Lancia Smith poetically writes, 'a season that is highly wrought with both meaning and emotional peril . . . a place where there happens a quiet and gradual unveiling of our true condition'.[2] Perhaps it is a time when, in response to the insistence of being *with* others, loneliness becomes more gigantic than it needs to be as our aloneness is potentially over-emphasized, highlighted like a gargoyle on a shadowy church wall, making so many feel vulnerable.

As Christians we are called to relate to others, to go out towards those who need a gentle word, a spacious pause, a bear hug. What helps, the poet Malcolm Guite suggests, is the recognition that the true peace and joy of Christmas is itself a gift, not something we can artificially produce or manufacture. If we are lucky enough to have love, any love, in our lives then we are duty bound to be expansive, generous with it – to extend it outwards to the family of God in the world wherever we find ourselves. The preface in the wedding service tells couples that marriage 'enriches society and strengthen community'[3] – I tell them their love should be big enough to overflow like a tiered set of champagne glasses, to fill those which are empty, way below in the pecking order of loving relationships.

Perhaps this is why new monastic communities are springing up around the world in various forms, communities that offer something distinctive and more accessible, even allowable, than the traditional family unit. Shane Claiborne's Potter Street Community has gathered Christian people to live amid others who cannot escape a downtown and run-down neighbourhood in Philadelphia. This community provides inspiration to those within the neighbourhood itself who might be tempted to feel that the rest of the world has abandoned them. It is a witness for people with faith having a transformative effect on an area of former desolation and has become a globally networked community of prayer and inspiration, which perhaps Nicholas Ferrar's Little Gidding might have done had he lived in the digital age. Reflecting on what is family, Claiborne says:

> Biological family is too small a vision. Patriotism is far too myopic. A love for our own relatives and a love for the people of our own country are not bad things, but our love does not stop at the border.[4]

We may not be able to live in such a way, a way which challenges our sense of individuality, privacy and safety, but we quite like the idea that we ourselves could be included, lovingly absorbed into some kind of alternative family if we were committed enough. Or even if we were just lonely.

Nicholas Ferrar is a saint remembered not for one extraordinary act or sacrifice but rather for the modelling – living out – of an alternative way to live in his time, one which rejected all extraneous materialism and one which refused to find meaning in that which is ultimately vacuous. He took the gifts he had been given and built a way of life that, centuries later, would retain a vision that continues to inspire many others. Since the mid-1850s there has been some kind of community at Little Gidding. In recent history, from the 1970s until the 1990s, work was carried out on the main buildings, which had fallen into disrepair, and the Community of the Sower was established. Now the Friends of Little Gidding keep the memory of Nicholas Ferrar alive, planning pilgrimages, services and events to extend the vision of 'family' outwards to those who are interested. Ferrar House is the current retreat centre.

Prayer ideas

- Pray for retreat houses, those who work there and the haven they provide.
- Pray for those involved in new monastic communities.
- Pray for your own family.
- Pray for those who are lonely.
- Visit <www.littlegiddingchurch.org.uk>.

Nicholas
Bearer of gifts

All of us love receiving gifts, and Christmas is a bumper time for presents. As Advent has become increasingly frenzied I have found it tempting over the past few years not to think *that* carefully about the kind of present that might be most appropriate or appreciated by those I buy for. In fact, we all know the shadow side of gift-giving – the recycling of gifts given to us in past years that we don't like too much, as well as the piles of unwanted presents which have become a symbol of wasted time and energy. Each year those of us with any kind of material conscience attempt to think about how we could 'do' Christmas differently. Could we offer homemade presents? (I did this one year – people loved them but it was considerably time-consuming.) Or what about tiny gifts which are inexpensive but interesting and creative? (I did this too – people loved the fact that this was different but some seemed slightly disappointed there wasn't something more.) Or what about just giving a lump sum of money (the equivalent you would spend on all your friends and family) to charity – after all, do any of us really need anything these days? (I did this too but felt uncomfortable about being mean and perhaps appearing to be a bit 'over-worthy'!)

Who would have thought gift-giving could become so complicated in our sophisticated world? Yet over the years I have given and received a whole heap of unusual and different gifts. My sister-in-law presented me with a mosaic of the design of my first book (I was immensely touched because at the time the enormity of me becoming a published author seemed to go unnoticed among some of my family). My mother has produced some hand-crafted leather-covered scrapbooks (she is a bookbinder) and has produced a version of 'Desiderata' in calligraphy. And we have a family friend with quite limited resources who puts a huge amount of care into anything she gives.

Perhaps this latter example is the key. When people give with real care, mindful of the actual needs of those they give to, it makes a difference. Even when my son's godmother and her husband give money the notes are crisp and new, not only symbolic of the preciousness of their own financial resources but indicative of the fact that my son should also understand money as important and to be spent carefully. Anonymous giving is also good as we reflect on the pleasure and help it will hopefully provide for someone. Several years ago, when we were struggling with a large car maintenance bill, someone put £200 through our door. Although I tried hard, I never got to the bottom of who posted it, and being a person who likes to be grateful I found this slightly frustrating as well as humbling. Another year I mirrored this act of kindness by doing the same (not quite as much money!) to someone I knew who was in need around Christmas time when I had some spare cash from a ministerial job I had participated in.

We have a saying in our family that sometimes a gift seems to reflect the tastes and personality of the giver rather than the person receiving it. Perhaps we have all been guilty of this in the past – we choose things to give to others that we would quite like ourselves rather than thinking our way into the desires and hearts of the person we are buying for. This is what the Wise Men (whom we also remember in this book) *didn't* do, for their gifts were highly 'Jesus-specific', gifts which resonated with the man–God he was and would become. Person-centred presents – most definitely!

Nicholas is a saint we remember on 6 December. He was born into a wealthy family in the third century. His parents died young but had raised Nicholas as a devout Christian. Obeying Jesus' command-ments to go and sell what he owned and give away the proceeds to the poor he used his *entire* inheritance to help the vulnerable, sick and suffering in the area where he lived. He subsequently dedicated his life to serving the God he loved and was made Bishop of Myra while still a young man. His kind and loving nature established his reputation of generosity throughout the region, as well as his love and concern for children, sailors and ships. Interestingly, Nicholas is also the patron saint of shoppers, so at the beginning of Advent it seems highly appropriate to remember him. Under the Roman emperor Diocletian, Nicholas suffered for his faith, was exiled and imprisoned, but on release attended the Council of Nicaea in AD 325. Legend has it that when he died a liquid substance called manna was found in his grave; this was said to have healing properties, which increased his popularity, and many legends have sprung up as a result.

Perhaps the most famous story associated with Nicholas is his helping of a poor man who had three daughters. Providing three substantial dowries for these young women was not an option and without it the girls were unlikely to find husbands. They faced instead a life of slavery and potential prostitution. The story goes that on three different occasions a bag of gold was thrown through an open window, landing in the women's shoes and stockings which had been left by the fire to dry. The father was therefore able to provide a sufficient dowry for each of his daughters. This is why we have the tradition of leaving stockings out on Christmas Eve, hoping that in the morning they will be filled with delight-inducing presents! Three gold balls are sometimes depicted in pictures of St Nicholas as symbols of these three bags.

There are also connections here between the tiny things of the kingdom that Jesus continuously used as metaphors to describe God's alternative vision for the world: mustard seeds, salt, yeast and sparrows, to name but a few. Maybe 'keep it simple' is a good mantra for us as Christians, to try to find imaginative ways of simultaneously marking the season with a genuine spirit of generosity while somehow trying to dissolve the intense and oppressive materialism that hits us like a train. I long for us to be much more creative with our gift-giving – perhaps promising someone some quality time, an afternoon out, a mystery tour, a listening ear or help with the garden. These are just a few of the imaginative ways of empowering those with few material resources to think of 'gifts' they could nevertheless give which would make a difference to another's life, things which cost nothing but some love and time, perhaps that most precious commodity of all. As Christian communities we can model an alternative way to 'do Christmas' which provides an antidote to the tide of consumerism and replaces it with soothing calm and manageability.

Gerald Vann offers some interesting thoughts on an appropriate approach to materialism, explaining that while we have a proper expectation to property and possessions as humans, we must always understand that with this comes a duty to others.

> We have a right to property, yes; but every right implies a corresponding duty. The right to property implies a duty to the common

good – and the more we have, the greater our responsibility for that common good. We have a right to property, but only within the life of charity. And as with material possessions of every sort, so with all that we have and are, the gift enables us to be humbly and royally lavish, and above all with the gift of pity itself. You must be lavish, first of all, to those nearest to you, those you love most; but you must be lavish, too, to those who are most in need.[1]

A contemporary website recounts inspiring and touching stories of unusual Christmas 'gifts' given to others. One was a letter written by a ten-year-old, hidden behind the Christmas tree and opened after all the other presents had been unwrapped. It was a genuine expression of love and gratitude to her parents for their care. The mother was so touched by this unexpected gift that she framed the hand-written letter and hung it on the wall of her bedroom. Another family tell the story of a period when they were very short of money through sickness and inability to work. The family had just had a new baby and had another young toddler as well as two teenagers. Prior to Christmas, the church office called and asked the wife to make up a 'wish list' of gifts for the whole family. A couple of weeks later the family received a phone call to say that there were several presents waiting for them in the office, including a cheque for money to pay the bills and purchase good food for the Christmas dinner.[2] Definitely person-centred presents here!

Alternative ways to give this Christmas

- Give homemade presents on a theme.
- Give tiny gifts (you could always give money and vouchers as well).
- Buy gifts from charities which provide resources in other countries.
- Offer gifts of help such as gardening, babysitting, listening, shopping, taking someone for a day out or a treat.
- As a church, identify people who will really struggle in your church or wider community. Arrange for a Secret Santa to help. One family could provide a gift for another family, one individual for another.
- Pray during Advent that we become more generous as individual people of faith as well as a Christian community.

Ambrose
When in Rome, do as the Romans do

Most people reading this book will have a favourite prayer, hymn or section in the liturgy. Some too will remember a time when God spoke to them through words or music, helpfully, maybe profoundly, at a time when their heart was, for whatever reason, especially receptive. Anglicans reading this will understand that the varied richness of the liturgy is at the very centre of a worshipping tradition that has gone back centuries, from the Book of Common Prayer to the now infinite varieties of *Common Worship* with all its seasonal choices.

Ambrose began his life as Bishop of Milan after an unlikely start. A political leader, he was appointed as bishop in 374 by popular demand after the death of the previous leader, when a fracas had arisen between the Catholics and a faction known as the Arians.[1] After a brief period in hiding, believing that he was not worthy, Ambrose consented to become the new bishop. Within a week he was baptized, ordained and duly consecrated as the city's ecclesial leader – a swift vocational path – and became one of the most influential ecclesiastical figures of the fourth century. While Arianism raged among the ruling elite, Ambrose sought to oppose this unorthodox belief, which was contrary to the Nicene Creed. He remained faithful to his position for centuries amid much pressure from those in power, who demanded the takeover of several churches in Rome as 'Arian' churches.

Throughout his ministry, Ambrose resisted the bullying pressure of those in authority who were unimpressed by his stoical and immovable principles of faith. As bishop, he excommunicated brutal leaders such as Theodosius for the killing of 7,000 people at Thessalonica in 390 after the murder of the resident Roman governor, only allowing him back after a suitable period of penance. Ambrose was no pushover: he was a holy man who adopted an ascetic and celibate lifestyle early on in his bishopric, often giving away his land

and money to the poor. No anaemic hermit, he stood like an ancient oak tree in the middle of a battlefield of heresy, remaining resolute beside the doctrinal principles he believed were the foundations of the Church and right belief.

Yet Ambrose also displayed a contrasting flexibility when it came to liturgical practice, believing passionately that liturgy should be a tool to serve people in worshipping God – a perspective which perhaps sounds strangely contemporary. Liturgy, he believed, should not become a rigid formula but a language which has the breathing space to be shaped by place and congregation. He advised Augustine of Hippo to follow liturgical custom: 'When in Rome, I fast on a Saturday; when in Milan, I do not. Follow the custom of the church where you are if you want to avoid giving scandal.'[2] Ambrose refused to be manipulated as to which liturgy and format was superior as he travelled, and his advice has lived on in the popular saying, 'When in Rome, do as the Romans do.'

Ambrose was also a writer of psalms and hymns and he is reputed to have been the initiator of the antiphonal or responsorial chant known as the 'Ambrosian chant', where the two sides of a choir alternately respond to each other. He is said to have composed the *Te Deum* (at the point when he baptized St Augustine) and is sometimes credited with the authorship of the *Exultet*, the hymn sung at the Easter Vigil as the Easter candle is processed into a dark church. He wrote a great deal of original hymnody, including four hymns which survive today written in eight four-line stanzas. Among other things, Ambrose is patron saint of beekeepers because he developed a reputation for his gentle and articulate preaching ability, gaining the nickname of 'Honey-tongued Doctor'.

At Christmas many of our churches will be filled with people who are unused to the sacred language of worship. Like the characters around the stable, this will most probably be a feisty mixture of folk from our own locality as well as those who are visiting from further afield. Our congregations mirror a diversity from articulate and educated voices just like the Wise Men to more localized people, integral to our towns and villages as represented in the shepherds. People will come and attend services, open and expectant to hear and be reassured that God is still alive and well in our world, which brings a golden opportunity for all who care about evangelism. The language we use in church is asked to be different from the language and speech of the everyday, distinctive and nudging us into the numinous. But it has to be understood by contemporary people in order to connect the big story of God with the little stories of our own lives. Through its metaphors and imagery, its poetry and beauty, such language needs the capacity to take us to a different level of existence.

Liturgy not only inspires us to think about divine things but potentially enables us to step through the veil of the ordinary into the grace and mystery of the person that God is. Like music, liturgy at its best can become a 'common language' that inspires us to dance rather than plod. It marks the fact that the function of worship, however and wherever it is done, is to direct our hearts and minds to honouring and loving God. One of the strengths of the Church of England is the great breadth of both ancient and contemporary liturgy. The Book of Common Prayer, still its official prayer book, unpacks theology with great depth, its specific and archaic language still memorized and valued by a great many Anglicans. *Common Worship* boasts eight eucharistic prayers and a vast spectrum of possible variations not just for Sunday worship but for specific festivals, as well as containing varied patterns for personal prayer. With this comes the idea that there is commonality as well as breathing space to mould and shape holy language to fit the needs of people in a cultural and social context.

Perhaps we stress too much that the language we use in church feels outdated, belonging to a culture we are no longer part of. Yet in our lives we often come up against contrasting 'cultures', whoever we are and wherever we are from. The 2004 film *Ladies in Lavender* recounts the story of Andrea, a gifted Polish violinist, who is swept overboard from a ship bound for America and washed up on a beach in Cornwall. Two sisters, Ursula and Janet, take him in. Although it soon becomes evident that Andrea speaks no English, his exquisite music becomes the universal and flexible language that not only establishes relationships but helps him integrate into the tight-knit Cornish village he has inadvertently become a part of. Good liturgy, like good music and Shakespeare's plays, is understood as something we work at a little, for within is to be found profound and universal truth as well as an eloquence that never dates. Language comes to us in many forms and it is a humble admittance to recognize that we will never fully articulate the person who is God. Perhaps this was at the heart of Ambrose's belief that we should tread carefully and lightly, not insisting on being too dogmatic in any liturgical practice.

In the Catholic Church the *Te Deum* itself is a *flexible* hymn. It is used on a variety of ceremonial occasions such as the election of a pope or bishop, the canonization of a saint and the publication of a treaty of peace. But it is also sung as part of the traditional and ordinary office, used at various stages throughout the church year. It follows the framework of the Apostles' Creed and is a combination of a poetic vision of heaven and a statement of faith – perhaps something of the essence of the person who was Ambrose. Ambrose said, 'Let no word pass your lips in vain, no meaningless word be uttered,' a cogent reminder that as followers of Jesus we should be people of careful speech, and theology too.[3] His advice to be flexible and follow the custom of the place wherever we find ourselves is also about retaining an open approach to fellow believers – of being gracious to the customs and practices of other Christians, even if occasionally they clash with our own. As worshipping people, we need to be open to the Spirit speaking to us in a myriad different styles, theologies and words, and over the past few decades communities specializing in grounded and more contemporary liturgies, such as Iona and the Northumbria Community, have become more mainstream. During four years working in a large evangelical church some years ago I developed a new appreciation of singing choruses or 'worship songs'. Initially struggling with the belief that these did not contain the profounder depths of theology or poetry that traditional hymns hold, over time I learned a new appreciation of their melodies and simplicity which became like prayers or contemporary chants – something I continue to value.

Prayer ideas

- Pray for all involved in writing liturgy and corporate prayer.
- Pray for a spirit of creativity in your own church context and prayer life.
- Pray for those with speech impediments.
- Pray for those in the diplomatic service and those who act as mediators.

Lucy
New eyes

For New Year in 2015 my family and I spent four days in northern Finland. Prior to our departure, a geography teacher friend told us that the sun officially went down in Ivalo (our destination) on 4 December and would not re-emerge until around 8 January. Our experience mirrored this. It was just about light at 10.00 a.m. and by 2.30 p.m. the grey cloud was fast deteriorating into gloom again. The sky carried a kind of heaviness characteristic of such snow-filled lands, and sadly the Northern Lights were not visible to us during our visit. Of course, Scandinavians are used to this but I cannot imagine living my entire day with so much in darkness.

Advent falls at a dark time of year. Our daylight hours are brief and before Christmas we hit the shortest day. As residents of the northern hemisphere we remember that we are people who respond to the light as we struggle to get out of bed on cold and sullen mornings. As people of faith we know that such an experience is part of a spirituality of waiting, anticipating the events of Christmas. Over the centuries, theologians have reflected on the fact that we need the darkness in order to understand the power of a light which is divine – Jesus, the Light of the World. As contemporary human people walking through December we encounter a visual feast of witty window displays and civic decorations in our villages and towns. Perhaps more than at any other time of year we enjoy this optical feast, challenging the child within us all to relive the magic moments of those first wondrous Christmases with all their neon exuberance and bright hope.

Those of us who have functioning sight are grateful for it, but as with many gifts our gratitude remains parked on the shelves of everyday forgetfulness. Those people who cannot see or have impaired vision speak of a heightened awareness of their other senses, the acute 'sensing' of life that most of us understand primarily through the ocular. But the wonder of the pre-Christmas season challenges us all to look at the world with fresh eyes – to see more within, to see something different in what might appear ordinary or boring or unbeautiful to others. Jesus' challenge to those who followed him was to look at the world of earthly reality and to discern, notice, sense a beauty within it which points to the reality of God, a beauty which can only be discernible through a grace-filled attitude to the world. Canon Douglas Rhymes captures this well:

> The meeting of Christ in us with the Christ in others will mean that we shall be willing to expose ourselves in openness to others without fear, seeing each person we meet as having a significance because both of us are accepted and loved by God. To have a prayerful approach to people is to have eyes to see, a mind intent upon seeing, a heart hopeful of seeing the image of God in each person I meet, to see them in themselves and in God.[1]

St Lucy, whose feast we celebrate on 13 December, knew all about sight. A native of Syracuse in Sicily, she lived at the beginning of the fourth century when the Roman authorities were attempting to re-establish the worship of their own gods. Legend has it that as a new Christian, Lucy gave away her possessions to the poor and was betrayed by her angry fiancé, who informed the authorities of her rebel faith. The Roman governor, Paschasius, tried to force defilement upon her by imprisoning her in a brothel, but the guards who came to take her away found they could not move her. Neither did she respond to burning, until finally she died by the sword. But Lucy has become famous for enduring the horrific removal of her eyes, after she warned Paschasius that he would be punished by God for his evil intent. The legend also tells that while her body was being prepared for burial it was discovered that her eyes had been miraculously restored.

It is a terrible thing to be robbed of your sight or even to lose it naturally. A gruesome scene in the recent Bond film, *Spectre*, showed the villain blinding a victim with his bare hands. It is one of the ultimate acts of cruelty, stripping someone of both autonomy and individuality: our eyes are the windows of our souls. Those who know they are slowly losing their sight often have a heightened and intense sense of appreciation for the glory and gift which is our sight. Lucy's name in Latin means 'light' and she has become associated with the one true Light whom believers eagerly await as the redeeming hope of the world. In Sweden candlelit processions mark her festival.

Inspired by this brave saint, Advent can be a time when we are challenged to see the world with new eyes and refreshed sight, our heart seeing, sensing beyond, wondering at, the terrible beauty of a God who challenges us to use our eyes, minds and hearts with an alternative vision, to continually see the world through an alternative perspective. Ruth Burrows, a Carmelite nun, says this:

> Every human being is for God and has an openness for God. It is not only around us who know his name but around every single person that the sun is shining, seeking an entrance. He uses every occasion to illuminate us and his illumination is most often perceived as darkness. Dark and light are inextricably bound up; we cannot really experience the piercing brightness which is God without the experience of being surrounded by utter darkness.[2]

On Hove seafront each year 25 beach huts are transformed into a 'living Advent calendar' which owners decorate around a theme such as 'Christmas carols'. It is a chance for local people to explore the poetry and theology in the age-old songs we sing as part of faith and culture throughout Advent, a fusion of secular and sacred marking and celebrating in a local context. Every evening one hut 'opens', just like a traditional Advent calendar window. Members of the community are invited to 'come and see', as well as to a variety of events linked with the displays, both social and spiritual. The beach hut advent calendar is linked to Beyond, a Church of England 'Fresh Expression' of church which explores monthly spiritual topics using art and discussion. It is a creative spin on a traditional idea but one which encourages people to come together through a community project and to undertake something of a journey with the dark backdrop of the ocean tide pounding in the background. Each evening, one more beach hut opens its display as the tableau grows, communicating that Advent is a time of waiting and expectancy, that the Christmas event is worth patience and pondering and that God only ever partially reveals his majesty and beauty to the world.

Beach huts are of course traditional 'small spaces' where people can enjoy temporary shelter from a too fresh wind on a typical British summer day. Over the last few years in coastal venues from Abersoch to Southend they have enjoyed something of a revival, in spite of their slightly precarious character and the new extremes of wind and storm our country has been subject to. They are places of strange comfort and shelter, adaptable spaces, as demonstrated in this project. Advent culminates in the occasion of another such adaptable space – the stable – a non-ideal venue for the birth of the Saviour of the world but one which nevertheless radiated with the warmth of a temporary community gathered around the beautiful and vulnerable child who was Jesus. This coming was unexpected, stimulated by the 'big visuals' of exuberant angels in the sky, trumpeting their heavenly message to a quiet hillside and unassuming shepherds. But the scene by the manger is also one of quiet and meditated wonder – where the simple and levelling beauty of a new baby enables all who gaze upon him to see this beauty, to be inwardly transformed, even for a moment.

The beach huts have a practical purpose but during Advent they become something quite different which keeps the rumour of God alive. The gift God gives to every human person is the gift of our life, our 'being'. The gift he asks in return is our 'becoming' – that we grow into people inhabited by the wonders of him. As Christians waiting for the *coming* again, we are people who understand this becoming, this movement to grow into a community of people who know they are the beloved of God, people who really see and believe with light in their eyes, people alive with God. This is partly a mystery as it unfolds in our lives – we are not always able to perceive the beauty within ourselves or others. There is something about the notion of hiddenness as Jesus was concealed in Mary's womb for nine months, the significance of who he was shrouded from the world. The beach huts hide the wonder of their displays until it is their day to open, until finally all are open, to reveal a unique and glorious tableau of ravishing beauty and theological meaning.

In his book *Celebrating the Saints* Robert Atwell quotes from Clement of Alexandria, on St Lucy's feast day:

> The commandment of the Lord shines clearly, giving light to the eyes. 'Receive Christ, receive power to see, receive light that you may recognise in him both God and man'. More delightful than gold and precious stones, more desirable than honey from the honeycomb is the Word that has given us light. How could he not be desirable, he who illuminated minds buried in darkness, and endowed with clarity of vision the light-bearing eyes of our souls? Let us open ourselves to

the light, and become disciples of the Lord. Sing your Father's praises, then, Lord, and make him who is God known to me. Your words will save me; your song will instruct me. Until now I have gone astray in my search for God but you are light for my path, and in you I find God.[3]

Advent calls us to reinhabit our usual spaces and places and to see them and the world in renewed wonder, with defined vision. This possibility lies in our own preparedness to relive this season with fresh eyes and hearts, just as Mary is knocked off her feet by a new and extraordinary event which brings her to life in a totally new way, giving her a completely new direction. For us, then, it is about refusing to make this season an inward groan, a chore, a material headache, a joyless, rushed and insignificant month. It is about relishing the opportunity to see God coming to earth again, cutting through a hopeless and sometimes cynical mindset with a renewed and holy vision.

Prayer ideas

- Pray for victims and perpetrators of torture and the work of organizations like Amnesty International.
- Pray for those who cannot physically see.
- Pray for opticians and eye surgeons who enable others to see.
- Pray for yourself – that you may sense the light of Christ in experiences of darkness and that you may be a person who shines light into the darkness of the world. Pray that you may see something of God within every person you meet.

Samuel Johnson
Moral messaging

Where do we formulate our moral code? What values do we live by if we are not a person of belief? Years ago, the Christian faith provided the moral backdrop for the majority of this country's citizens. Such faith was akin to a carefully woven tapestry hung on the walls of a person's life, a resource which could be contemplated carefully or simply ignored. But it was there, threaded through collective society. As enlightened life has evolved, scientific and rational philosophies have provided stimulating alternatives to the faith narrative. And as people with a learned individuality we have always had the choice of laying aside any belief systems and moral codes in the society of which we are a part. There have been plenty of people who, over the centuries, have been publicly seen to toe the political or faith 'party line' while secretly rejecting it.

Our ideologies are most often shaped by the context and communities we inhabit. As we journey through life, we learn to embrace, reject or develop these. Many of us try to do this solo, seeking the advice and wisdom of self-help books or flirting with a variety of quasi-religious philosophies which enable us to formulate some kind of rule for life and principles by which to live. Others just watch Jeremy Kyle and visit the default option of the Church of England when needs must. But lest I sound too cynical I believe that human nature is (usually) better than this; that deep within many is a yearning to live a good life, to contribute something to society and to develop some sense that the universe does not revolve entirely around us, that our lives revolve around something bigger.

Before our own era, saturated with visual and audio stimulation, came a slower age. The eighteenth century was one of great flourishing in terms of artistic and literary thought and production. Samuel Johnson was born into this age, the writer and moralist we commemorate on 13 December. Johnson, born in 1707, is perhaps best known as the compiler of the *Dictionary of the English*

Language. Educated at Lichfield and Oxford, Johnson was forced to leave university through lack of funds. He subsequently moved to London and over the years established a genuine and strong literary reputation. Johnson was a devout Anglican and his understanding of how to live out and communicate his faith remains a strand that runs through his writings.

His *Dictionary of the English Language* took him eight years to compile and was published in 1755. It proved to be the most important book of its time, running to six further editions. In 1763 Johnson met a Scottish lawyer, James Boswell, who championed the writer and helped his reputation to gain momentum. Johnson's dictionary was not the first but was the most commonly used for 150 years before the *Oxford English Dictionary* came into wider usage. According to American professor Jack Lynch, the book was 'a faithful record of the language people used. It is more than a reference book; it is a work of literature.'[1]

As well as this immense achievement, Johnson was a writer of essays, sermons and poems. His series *The Rambler* was an anonymous collection of essays on moral and religious topics which was hugely influential during his lifetime, and these essays were reprinted nine times. One of Johnson's most famous works is a poem entitled *The Vanity of Human Wishes.* In it the writer emphasizes 'the helpless vulnerability of the individual before the social context' and 'the inevitable self-deception by which human beings are led astray'.[2] Johnson scholar Donald Greene, commenting on Johnson's style, says that interestingly, for such a faith-based writer, his writings do not contain 'a premeditated and suggested pattern of behaviour – there is no prescriptive advice as to how to "be good" but more observations about the influence the world has on those who seek to live by alternative moral and religious rules'.[3] Perhaps Johnson's aim was to leave his readers not only touched and affected but stimulated to gently critique the 'values of the age' as well as being accountable for their own behaviour. Johnson was also always respectful of those of other denominations who followed Christ's teachings and he was known to be intolerant of Milton's more puritanical beliefs, believing these to be contrary to an English Christianity.

The Vanity of Human Wishes follows the Roman poet Juvenal's tenth satire. Johnson's poem has as its main theme the suggestion that we have a human tendency to ask for and expect all the wrong things in life – money, power, fame, military and political glory, longevity and beauty, to name a few. The bulk of the poem lists what the writer considers to be vain, advising people to stay away from 'surface pursuits'. These are folly and create a catalogue of vain desires leading to pride, greed and other vices which, taken to extremes, bring about an individual's downfall. Perhaps because of his strong and living faith, Johnson uses satire to exaggerate and emphasize social ills, as well as the vulnerability of the individual influenced and swayed by them, in an effort to connect with his readers. One modern critic attributes the poem's successful effect to 'the vigorous involvement between the narrator/writer and the reader'.[4]

Thanks to the development of electronic media, we live at a time when such a dynamic between writer and reader seems far easier to achieve and perhaps even more invigorating than it ever was. It is possible to put 'out there' our opinions about most things, to debate, to state, to critique, to formulate, albeit anonymously, what we might think about – well, *anything*. The rise of the digital age and the communication this involves has been much assessed and written about. One of the aims of a writer like Samuel Johnson is to stimulate people to work out what they think and believe, to formulate a healthy way to live both materially and spiritually. We live at a time when how we feel and what we think can remain unchallenged for the most part, unless we are committing some kind of crime. The religious and political leaders among us know that how we obtain and retain influence in the 'public space' has also changed dramatically over the past few decades. Lambasting, moralizing in a traditional sense, creating belief systems which are guilt-inducing – these no longer catalyse or persuade the average contemporary person. We need subtler ways to communicate the values we live by as people of faith, new ways of communicating how those values make a difference to our own and others' lives. Perhaps how *we* operate and how we do our ontological 'being' proves to be the most effectual tool we have.

On this note the work of Micah Purnell is simultaneously a comparison and a contrast to the messages that Samuel Johnson was trying to communicate through the medium of his various writings. Purnell is a Manchester-based artist who uses public space to produce large-scale advertisements with alternative images and messages, as an antidote and subversion to the consumerism which is at the heart of much traditional advertising. In his words, 'public space is dominated by a language that subtly invites desires and inculcates envy, greed and lust'.[5] In a contemporary vein Purnell mirrors the work and aims of Johnson in his poem, not only inviting his observers to reflect on the messages advertising instils but hoping that the individual will also challenge them. One such large billboard reads simply, 'Shackled by my own consumption', inviting passers-by to stop and think about their own presence and purpose in a city retail centre. Both Johnson and Purnell use statement, choice and gentle critique as a subversive tool to sway and stimulate a new or revised moral backdrop. Both use their Christian faith as an alternative message of hope in a world drenched by deadening values which are potentially toxic for the soul.

Advent is a time in the year when we are bombarded by visual and other imagery, to influence our material choices. Television advertisements supposedly promote good moral values (last year's John Lewis advertisement centred on the fact that no one should be alone at Christmas) and yet behind the sentimental messages lies the lurking demon of consumerism, of promoting a specific shop and the lifestyle wrapped up with this. While enjoying the festivities and joy of genuine giving, most people of faith sense that the message behind the Christmas story has far-reaching implications in terms of a bigger heartbeat of service and love, asking us to reassess the alluring media messages, seductive adverts and everything that tempts the materialist and consumerist parts of ourselves. The Incarnation reminds us that we must never lose sight of seeing God in those most on the edge of society, those who are pushed out and laid aside by societal forces, and we can make Advent a time when we decisively challenge the values and messages of our age and dance to a different tune.

Prayer ideas

- Pray for artists and writers who challenge the values of the age.
- Pray for Christian artists and writers.
- Pray for all who work with language, for speech therapists and all who help people with the gift of speech.
- Pray for politicians, clergy and all public figures who influence others through what they say, and for those you know personally.

John of the Cross
Our deepest yearning

John of the Cross is a giant of a saint. And like many giants he seems, to many a contemporary Christian, difficult to understand. There are too many aspects to his spirituality to focus on in a short reflection, but suffice it to say his legacy has had a profound and far-reaching effect on the history of spirituality from its origins in the sixteenth century right up to its implications for our parched twenty-first-century souls.

John de Ypres (who adopted his more familiar name later) was born in Spain in 1542, into a noble but impoverished family. John was brought up by his widowed mother and educated at a charity school; he briefly worked as a nurse before entering the Carmelite Order when he was 21. He studied to be a priest at Salamanca University, where he met Teresa of Avila. Teresa was in the process of reforming the order by setting up small communities committed to poverty and simplicity, and where members lived under principles of extreme equality – a radical way of living at a time when social and material status was of the utmost importance for most of the population. Teresa proved an inspirational figure for John, who joined her reformed movement. They shared much in common in their approach to prayer and passionate yearning for God, believing that the real fulfilment of the human life was to be united with God through love. John founded the first 'discalced' monastery at Duruelo in 1568 and continued to found seven more across Andalusia.[1]

John's life was marked by suffering, which became the deep well where much of his theology was formulated. He was imprisoned in 1577, having become a target for Carmelites who were opposed to the discalced reform movement, believing it too austere. John was shut away at a monastery in Toledo, locked in a tiny room which had little natural light and was perishingly cold in winter and suffocatingly hot in summer. He had little to eat or drink and was regularly flogged and mentally tormented, but eventually he managed to escape, finding refuge with the nuns at Toledo. He went on to build more communities but his suffering continued: he was removed from the office of Vicar-Provincial in 1591, as he continued to be a champion for the reforms promoted by Teresa for the Carmelite Order.

The hardness and suffering which characterized John's life and faith were instrumental in his fascination for and exploration of spiritual darkness, where he felt acutely the absence of God. John's spirituality is well known for the 'dark night' – the bleak terror of feeling that God is somehow absent rather than present in our life struggles and troubles, however this is manifested. Yet behind this is John's deepest desire and belief – that the purpose of every human life should be a deep union with God. Throughout his writings he laments that so many are simply not interested in this, perhaps for us too a strangely contemporary sorrow. Essentially he challenges his readers: why do human beings spend so much time and energy on things that don't matter, things which seem shallow and meaningless? Union with God for John is learning to see the world as God does, to be immersed in a love so profound and so expansive that we begin to see the world with the same love and compassion, which John expresses in his powerful poem *The Living Flame of Love*.

> Flame, alive, compelling,
> Yet tender past all telling,
> Reaching the secret centre of my soul!
> Since now evasion's over,
> Finish your work, my Lover,
> Break the last thread, wound me and make me whole![2]

The poem's further words stress the intense yearning John has for God to overtake the whole of him, to break him and wake him up, to flood his being with a single-minded and intense desire for God, where 'the touch of God is like a wound, an ache of desire to be made whole in him.'[3]

As we have already stated, much of John's spirituality stems from the concept of darkness, and darkness is what happens at night. Night time is a period when most of us sleep, a state from which we also need to wake. John calls us to wake up to the abundance and persistence, beauty and depth of God's love. He calls us to wake up to the transforming effect such love has on us, if we allow it, to fill our being and to re-orientate the approach to our life and work. With this comes a joy and mystery so deep it often proves unfathomable for the majority of faithful people. John's experience of suffering is the catalyst for this deep yearning to be united with God simply because, within it, God feels so absent.

On the one hand John's spirituality is thorny and tough and perhaps runs against our contemporary tendency towards a soothing spirituality which reassures and self-helps. My tendency is often to look to God for easy answers, reassurance, tangible presence rather than to live with the mystery of absence, doubt, failure and the possibility that God does at times remain silent and passive in my so-important life. Yet it is, I believe, also possible to sense the often indecipherable and unspoken yearning for a meaningful love at the heart of our own society. As a priestly leader I also yearn for the promotion of a spirituality which allows people to question where and why God feels absent, a spirituality which copes with, even relishes, difficult theological problems. For it feels far more real, as well as honest, to face these questions rather than hear the often slick platitudes we sometimes deliver as pastoral care or from the pulpit.

For the yearning to love, to be filled with love in order to love more, as well as the experience of the absence of God in situations of continuing suffering and darkness, must be respected, accompanied and courageously faced even when, like St John, we struggle to find an easy faith through it. Yet recognizing such a state is when we spiritually 'wake up' and grow up too. If we can be brave enough to face the fog then such wrestlings can be times of spiritual growth, when God's grace is working through us through agony or disbelief, 'pulling us towards fulfilment, not emptiness, towards beauty and life, not annihilation'.[4] As Rowan Williams comments, 'Christian experience does not simply move from one level to the next and stay there, but is drawn again and again to the central and fruitful darkness of the cross'.[5] But in this continuous movement and yearning there is life and growth, like new buds stretching out their leaves from a winter's branch.

Advent and Christmas are times when many sense the 'God-shaped hole' within themselves. Many come back to church, hopeful for words of spiritual reality. For those who lead as well as welcome it is an opportunity to preach and share something which resonates with the reality of so many people's lives as these are lived in hardship or a lack of genuine and faithful love, and perhaps with an under-developed and infantile understanding of what the Christian faith is really about. Edgar Allison Peers, who translated John's writings, described John's theology as like a medicine – tonic and astringent rather than an emollient or sedative.[6] John encourages believers to move past the sweetness of a sense of tangible presence and to progress, learning to trust in God even when he might appear to be absent. We grow spirituality in deepening our faith, in learning to trust more whenever we find ourselves in the middle of the desert when there seems nothing of God's presence and no signs of encouragement. For John, mature faith is about dwelling in and growing through the darkness because of our own yearning for a love for and meeting with God.

I have just finished reading Kasuo Ishiguro's latest novel, *The Buried Giant*, a book ten years in the writing. The plot centres around two ancient Britons, Axl and Beatrice, who journey out of the safe environment of their village to search for the son who left years ago. Their journey is full of adventure and they are incapacitated by a strange mist which lies like a foggy blanket over the whole land, a dragon's breath, the result of a spell cast by Merlin to cloud people's memories. And so they travel in faith and trust, through hardship and darkness, and throughout, their own depth of love sustains their not always light-filled relationship. The fog Axl and Beatrice battle with reminds me of the metaphorical darkness and confusion so many of us feel on a variety of levels within our own lives. But such darkness is as much a part of reality as any easy and illuminated pathway. Love is often what sustains us through life, giving us the strength to continue, and for Axl and Beatrice it proves a sustenance which keeps them going forward unflinchingly, even amid the brutal honesty of their own relationship. As with most darkness and confusion, eventually the mist disperses and a new adventure opens up as they too 'grow up', parting company when Beatrice is taken over to an island by a mysterious ferryman, alone.

Our own spiritual journeys, too, ultimately must be undertaken alone, but along the way, in darkness and in light, we find sustenance and hope in the yearning to love one another and our God, however imperfectly.

Prayer ideas

- Pray for those who are imprisoned, abused and tortured.
- Pray for those in spiritual darkness and struggling to find faith.
- Pray for religious communities, especially the Carmelites.
- Pray for those who promote and teach prayer and spirituality.

Eglantyne Jebb
Save the Children

As a mother, I have what my daughter describes as 'the need to feed' and I am now blessed with having two children who eat anything save mushrooms and avocados. I will take some of the credit for this – as a genuine 'foodie' I have encouraged them to experiment and taste a variety of good food and to understand the physical as well as spiritual joy of both cooking and eating well. My 13-year-old son especially has developed a genuine openness to the exotic, loving unusual seafood and even trying fried tarantula once on holiday in Cambodia! Some of this is, of course, because we live in an age of food plenty – we are saturated and satiated by overwhelming culinary choice. Most of us living in the United Kingdom today are 'so fortunate' – a moral cliché, but it is also sobering to remember that my mother, a child of the war, still remembers the time when she saw her first banana.

No one likes to see hungry kids. It's distressing but sadly still prevalent in a world which statistically produces enough food to feed everyone. In December, a time when we concentrate much on plentiful, luxury food, in our own country at least, it seems poignant that one of the holy people we remember is Eglantyne Jebb, the founder of Save the Children. Eglantyne was born into a well-off family in Shropshire in 1876 and her family were involved in much social action. After a typically genteel education appropriate for a single and respectable woman, Eglantyne was asked to travel to Europe on behalf of the Macedonian Relief Fund, returning just before the First World War broke out. She became involved in a project organized by her sister Dorothy, resulting in a growing knowledge that poverty was dire and growing in many countries in Europe. As hostilities came to an end, the sisters saw the horrific effects of the war which, coupled with the Allied blockade, meant that thousands of children in countries like Austria and Hungary were literally starving to death. The sisters responded by setting up the Save the Children Fund, with Eglantyne enlisting the help of a young London doctor, Hector Munro. Munro travelled to Vienna and brought back distressing reports of children dying in the streets and babies being thrown into the Danube or left to die in hospitals through a lack of food and medical treatment for malnutrition.

Rightly disturbed by this, Eglantyne approached the Archbishop of Canterbury, aiming to grow national support through the Anglican Church. Shockingly, the Archbishop declined. Undaunted, she approached the Pope. Pope Benedict XV was a lonely figure and the war had brought him an ambiguous reputation. Perhaps because of this he jumped at the chance of contributing in a positive way to the aftermath of the war. The Pope arranged for food and clothing collections to be made in Roman Catholic churches all over Europe and supported this by writing a subsequent Encyclical, mentioning Save the Children by name and insisting that any help should not show favour to Catholic children alone. This course of action galvanized (and perhaps shamed) the Archbishop to also act through the Church of England.

Yet the emergency feeding and care of children was not Eglantyne's lasting contribution. Her work is perhaps akin to that of those who not only undertake to set up food banks today but also seek to ask searching questions of any government as to why such ventures are necessary in a developed and sophisticated country. She was passionate too about protecting the poorest of the poor through sound legislation to make sure this section of society did not slip below the poverty line.

The culmination of Eglantyne's work was the Declaration of the Rights of the Child, a children's charter also known as the Geneva Declaration, which was written in 1924 and rapidly adopted by the League of Nations. This was perhaps something of a precursor to the idea that children are not simply the private property of their own family but that society as a whole bears responsibility for every child's well-being. Preaching at the Declaration's ratification in Geneva, Eglantyne asked for the inspiration of her God, that he might promote a continuous striving to sweep away for ever 'this iniquitous child suffering'.[1] Among many things the Declaration of the Rights of the Child advocated that every child should be fed and have adequate healthcare, that orphans should be cared for and 'the backward' children helped. Children should be protected from every form of exploitation but helped to earn a living when necessary, and every child should have adequate means to develop both physically and spiritually. Eglantyne was also keen that children themselves should develop a sense that they have something to contribute to the society that has nurtured them, a 'consciousness' behind many an organization such as the Guides or the Duke of Edinburgh's Award Scheme.

Over the last 20 years in our own country it feels that such 'rights' have become moulded into a firmly set stone. Some people of faith baulk against the idea of 'rights', insisting rather that everything we receive is to be understood as 'gift' and grace from a loving God. But we also know that without Eglantyne's prophetic Declaration many children the world over would have fared much worse than they have in recent years. Rights are necessary, but perhaps, as people of faith, we are called to approach them from an alternative perspective. Now for us in the generally wealthy Western hemisphere, there can be a tendency to create idols out of our children – they must always come first, on Sundays the extracurricular activities they have chosen usually come before going to church, as parishioners often apologetically explain to me, perhaps to appease their guilt. How children *feel* and whether they are happy can become an obsession, and our own children's educational needs are sometimes savagely fought for against others' in terms of school places.

But Christmas time is one season when we can rebalance the scales of parental responsibilities as we think about children who will not wake up on Christmas Day to a pile of presents. Most parents, like me, have participated in Christmas schemes like the Shoebox appeal, where boxes are filled with toys and school equipment to send to those who do not even have the basics like socks and pencils. But although worthy, this is hardly sacrificial for any of us who inhabit lives which are fairly comfortable. Eglantyne Jebb was never a mother. She demonstrates a whole life offered to the championing of a cause which was nothing to do with her own needs or any desires she might have had to be a parent herself.

It remains a powerful witness to read of people who feel the call to take on the nurture and care of those for whom they ultimately have no responsibility. People such as these model what was so crucial to Eglantyne herself – that our responsibility as human beings is to have a wider remit, to understand that our lives are not simply to be lived in the private domain, caring for our friends and family only, but that we have a relationship to all people and that we are ultimately all connected. Recently the *Church Times* featured an inspiring article about a contemporary Eglantyne Jebb, Faith Uwantege, a deeply Spirit-filled woman who has built a school and created an educational foundation in the Rwandan village where she lives. Starting with just one impoverished family who did not have enough to eat, Faith visited them daily and was inspired to gather funding and resources from people she met, as well as garnering international support. She led by example, investing all of her personal savings in the project before asking for help from others. After buying a plot of land, Faith now has 35 people building the school where she already teaches, largely parents of the children themselves who can see the difference education makes. The venture is called the Faith Foundation and the teaching of her 160 children happens alongside the physical construction of the school. As the lawyer and journalist Albert Pike said, 'What we have done for ourselves alone dies with us; what we have done for others and the world remains and is immortal.'[2]

Jesus came into the world initially as a child with a temporary home, vulnerable as a refugee in a strange land, where his own life was in danger. He becomes a symbol of hope to the many thousands of hungry and lonely street children and young people who work long hours in physically or morally dangerous conditions in order to survive. The spirit of Advent and Christmas lies here in the tatty and blood-soaked swaddling cloths wrapped around him, a message which extends outwards to all who find themselves in such a position. Theologian Paul Rowntree Clifford reminds us that it is part of all Christian evangelism to remember that every human person born on this planet has 'the very hairs of their heads numbered', that 'all people are of inestimable value because they are children of God, the concern of His love, created for an eternal destiny, not just people in general, but individuals, each with a name, each having priceless worth'. He goes on to say that if the imagery that Christ himself uses is true, then the significance of these words is far-reaching, that

> if God really does care for every single man, woman and child in the teeming millions that inhabit the globe . . . we cannot dismiss anyone as of no consequence, nor are we entitled to suppose that some are more important than others or that any should be sacrificed to serve some interest which takes precedence over their inherent worth.[3]

Eglantyne's legacy was to challenge our obsession with our ever-shrinking personal spheres of existence and to care and work passionately for the rights of all who are not privileged in the things our own children automatically enjoy.

Prayer ideas

- Pray for street children, and for children who are hungry and homeless everywhere and those who work with them.
- Pray for the work of Save the Children.
- Visit <www.faithfoundation.rw/index-1.html>.

CHRISTMAS SAINTS

John the Baptist
Unlikely prophet

———◆◆◆———

John the Baptist – cherished and extraordinary child of Elizabeth and Zechariah, both far beyond child-bearing years. Mary and Elizabeth experience both joy and terror as we imagine them mulling over the enormity of the implications of bearing God-inspired children.

As Advent is a season of preparation – a time for the world to remember the impact of the Incarnation – there would be an aching, empty gap of meaning if John the Baptist were not to be considered in this book. For John is the one who prepares the way for God to decisively arrive in the world at Christmas in the form of a small child. John was a wild and weird man, perhaps a hermit, wearing animal skins and foraging what he could in desert places. He was possibly a member of the Jewish sect of the Essenes, a group of Jews who practised a rigorous ascetic life which included voluntary poverty and daily immersion to express repentance and discipline. The Essenes shared messianic and eschatological beliefs which help us to understand the straightforward attitude John takes to his listeners, including the Pharisees and the Sadducees who approached him for baptism.

John is an individual we might choose to ignore ourselves, pretending not to hear, turning away from his challenging message of repentance that crazily heralds the possibility of a new era. Strange in appearance, he was nevertheless single-minded in his insistence that his purpose was to prepare the way for one who was greater than he. The world and people's behaviour is not as God intended it to be – there is corruption, violence and hypocrisy. The people need to repent, turn themselves around to cleanse their lives to prepare for God's Messiah. He pulls no punches with the religious groups of the day, calling them 'snakes' and telling them that if they do not take baptism seriously they will be rooted out and rejected, just as bad wheat is thrown on the fire.

During Advent, the second Sunday is dedicated to John as well as to remembering the legacy of the prophets. 'Prophet' is perhaps not a concept twenty-first-century people understand any more. Traditionally such a person was someone who spoke by divine inspiration, a person who believed him or herself to be an interpreter of God. Maybe it is simply a kind of truthfulness which resonates with what we instinctively believe to be right, true, fair. The American theologian Walter Brueggemann famously talked about the 'prophetic imagination', where our charge as believers in Christ is to perceive and understand the 'alternative view' of God in the world and to imagine this into being through words of faith and acts of intention. A prophet, then, is someone who helps others to understand a way forward for the world which is future-orientated, without it feeling that this is a future defined and prescriptive. With the presence and message of John the Baptist there is a sense of this future unfolding, unfurling like the beautiful drama of a peacock's tail.

All the Gospel writers link the person of John with the metaphorical words from Isaiah: 'I am the voice of one crying out in the wilderness, "Make straight the way of the Lord," as the prophet Isaiah said' (John 1.23). John's Gospel has these words coming from John himself.

Prophets were not soothsaying fortune tellers who predicted the future, but individuals who simply 'named' (and often shamed) the reality of the present, including the injustices and corruption of the government of the day. Prophets were people whose words echoed the Word in truth and whose often small actions activated others to change. Words hold power, and it was precisely John's words which became a huge threat to Herod. The Jewish historian Josephus became interested in this, which is why he too recorded the life of John. Herod Antipas's insecurity about his own regal status meant that any murmuring about an alternative king would be squashed on the flimsiest excuse. He was anxious too that John's preaching would raise a rebellion, so when his daughter danced before him, in his drunken state he foolishly agreed to grant the girl anything she wished for. After a consultation of great evil with her mother, John's head arrived on a platter.

Over the last month, I have become interested in the life and death of the American war correspondent and photo-journalist James (Jim) Foley, whose death stirred global outrage, shock and astonishment when he was decapitated by ISIL in August 2014.

A video of the killing was briefly posted on the Internet. Raised a Catholic, Jim had previously lived his life in the service of others, but in the words of his mother Elaine, he found his vocation as a photo-journalist recording life in war zones and places of serious global danger. Imprisoned and tortured twice he went missing in 2012 and was not seen again until the terrifying posting on the Internet. Jim passionately believed that without his and others' 'truth' shown through the images he took, the world would not understand how dangerous many areas were, including the plight of the indigenous people living in such places. In a film made about his life and legacy his many friends and colleagues acclaimed his enormous moral and spiritual courage. His mother described how he gradually dispensed with all his possessions so that he could live a peripatetic life of fluid freedom. His was a single-minded witness, and the more suffering he saw the more committed he became. In an interview on the US news programme *Democracy Now*, Jim's father, Dr John Foley, stated that initially he could not comprehend why Jim had insisted on returning to Syria until he realized that his son had made commitments to people he had previously met there, as well as feeling a sense of deep loyalty that he 'had to be there to tell the story'.

Jim Foley's life was testimony to the prophetic. Through his work as a photo-journalist he illuminated for the world the real state of play in Syria, Afghanistan and many other countries which are wracked by regimes of terror and religious extremism. His life became deeply and symbolically sacrificial as, like John, he lost it partly because his work posed a threat to the existing regime. Several articles recount how Jim exercised his faith to support and sustain himself and others imprisoned with him – saying the rosary and praying five times a day in solidarity with his Muslim brothers who had also become political prisoners. Pope Francis likened the life and witness of Jim to that of John the Baptist, pointing out that martyrdom is not a thing of the past but that 'the martyrs of our times' are 'men, women, children who are being persecuted, hated, driven out of their homes, tortured, massacred'.[1]

Both John and Jim ended their days under an authority which had grown chillingly flippant in its attitude to the sacredness of an individual life. In a sermon on 6 February 2015, Pope Francis said this of John's death:, 'John ends his life under the authority of a mediocre, drunk and corrupt king, at the whim of a dancer and the vindictive hatred of an adulteress. That is how this great man ends his life.'[2] It is a human tendency (and weakness) to dislike hearing the truth, especially if such truth threatens an individual or collective identity and personal choice. Then the truth becomes not only propaganda but at its worst can be understood as 'blasphemy'. John's life and death contrast sharply with the precious nature of the birth of Christ and indeed every baby, and in the cosy sentiment of Christmas time we must not forget that behind the peaceful stable underlying danger lurked for Jesus and Mary and Joseph. John lost his life because of the message he proclaimed. Jim Foley too lost his life because of the brave message he communicated to the world and because he, like John, became a sacrificial lamb on the altar of the casual vengeance of those who were blinded by a twisted and corrupted religious faith.

At Christmas so many of the words we will speak, recite, sing and offer will be ones of beauty and grace, steeped in the glories of heaven and of hopeful possibility. The point of the prophetic presence is to warn, to correct that which is dark or becoming darker, moving further from the light of Christ. Two quotes from Quaker writers advocate the significance of the prophetic voice of the Johns and Jim Foleys of this world:

> The meek and mild mediocrity of most of us stands in sharp contrast to that volcanic, upheaving, shaggy power of the prophets, whose descendants we were meant to be.[3]

And:

> Every cycle has its prophets – as guiding stars; and they are the burning candles of the Lord to light the spiritual temple on earth, for the time being. When they have done their work, they will pass away; but the candlesticks will remain and other lights will be placed in them.[4]

Prayer ideas

- Pray for all who risk their lives to illuminate the real state of the world.
- Pray for an end to all regimes of terror and indoctrinations of hate.
- Pray for those who seek to negotiate with religious extremists.
- Pray for those who have lost loved ones who have 'disappeared'.

Elizabeth
Defying expectations

———◦◦◦———

In the months leading up to the birth of a child, most couples talk much about which name they will choose. As a clergy couple, my husband and I were fairly sure we wanted either biblical or saints' names for whatever children might come along. And Shakespearian ones, because we also love this part of our British history and literature! There seemed endless possibilities. Chloe? Naomi? Finally we settled on Eve Rosalind – Eve meaning 'life' and Rosalind from *As You Like It*. For our son, we chose Aidan – solid and tough Celtic saint who brought the Christian faith to the lands of the north. It continues to be popular to give children the names of relatives who have gone before, so our son bears the names of both his deceased grandfathers, Martin and John. In a similar vein, the continuation of the family name was important and so my daughter also has Thornton, my maiden name, as one of hers. It was similar at the time of Christ, so it is no surprise that in Luke's birth narratives Zechariah cannot quite stomach the message from the angel Gabriel that his son will have a completely different name and he is temporarily silenced for his astonished disbelief. But his son's God-given name – 'John' – in Hebrew means 'God is gracious and has shown favour'. Here was a distinctive and apposite name because of John the Baptist's prophetic role and task as forerunner of Jesus.

Elizabeth must have wondered what on earth was going on. The biblical text says she was old, and whatever this means, she was probably past menopause and technically no longer able to conceive. More grandmother than mother, she found herself in a place where she perhaps wished to go back in time, to be 20 years younger. Not to have children had shameful implications for women like her, and this is why she embraces the news with joyful acceptance as well as trepidation. When it is time for her baby to be born, Elizabeth stands firm on the name – 'No! His name is to be John!'

As contemporary readers we miss the courageous defiance of this. It would have been almost unheard of for a male child not to take a father's name, as well as unheard of for a mother to put her foot down. But Elizabeth's strength comes from elsewhere. Over the period of her pregnancy she has also sheltered an expectant Mary, perhaps escaping a shady reputation as the two who are unborn echo one another's greatness by leaping in their respective wombs. Many conversations of wondering and worry must surely have passed between these two unlikely cousins before the births of both John and Jesus.

Elizabeth, like Mary in a different way, defies expectations. No one thought that this older woman would be given the chance to have a child. No one would have thought she would be given her husband's silent voice to firmly tell of God's promise by steadfastly stating that her child – God's child – was to be called John, pointing to the favour God was showering on the world.

Advent, of course, is also about expectation – and defying it. Each December the Church proclaims to the world that even amid its darkness and pain, God, in the form of a tiny child, comes to bring hope and good news. This tiny child comes to present a new vision for a way of existence which gives life and not death. That message is so incredibly important that it needed some preparation, a time of repentance and heralding so that people would indeed have 'ears to hear'. This is the nature and purpose of John, whose path took such a different course from his family heritage.

The Bible is full of individuals and situations that defy expectations, and what a good thing that is. A good thing because through it God's action breaks into the world continuously, like lightning searing through a tree trunk. The Bible provides the whole big story of God defying the tiny, meagre and narrow-minded way we try to limit him and what he can do. At the feeding of the 5,000, 12 additional baskets of leftover food are collected; at the wedding of Cana there is a superfluity of rich wine; unpleasant tax collectors are transformed simply through being in Jesus' presence; and people who are nobodies are healed of their blindness and sickness. In our own lives it is always a good thing when we ourselves defy expectations too. As a schoolgirl I loved English but my teacher never quite believed in me. I took it upon myself to show her what I was made of, to work extremely hard, finally defying my own as well as her expectations of me by achieving an A grade for my A level.

It is therefore a part of human life to defy expectations – the person who recovers from cancer, the project desperately in need of funding where the money rolls in just at the last minute, the way that somehow life at times just pieces together against all odds. God has a proven track record of not only using unlikely people but turning upside down circumstances that appear hopeless. In the words of Jesuit writer Daniel Considine from 1924:

> Thank God for all he has done for you, and ask him to do still more. Try to widen your horizon. Expect great things from God, and he will give them to you. In your relations with him be always happy, joyful and trusting. You are not going back because you feel his presence less. The real test of advance is not feeling, but the soul deepening.[1]

In the ancient world being pregnant meant being confined, away from the eyes of the world, for several months. Elizabeth as well as Mary would have had ample time to mull over the momentous implications of their future motherhood, ample time for their souls to deepen, as Considine states, ample time to battle with the demons of anxiety and uncertainty.

Another reason Elizabeth proves such a powerful figure is her ability to accept that she is caught up in a story so much greater than her individual identity. Here is a stalwart and steadfast woman who, against the odds, carries the weight (quite literally) of her responsibility for the sake of God and the world. It seemed fitting in the year that celebrated the Queen's 90th birthday to make a connection with our monarch – another resilient and stoical woman who has lived a life of courageous and self-sacrificial leadership. The commemorative booklet *The Servant Queen* recorded particularly how this Elizabeth's faith has been a steady and grounding measure which has enabled her to remain resolute throughout the tumultuous events of not only the twentieth century but also her own personal life. Beginning her reign in the aftermath of two world wars, she has coped with further wars in the Gulf and the Falkland Islands and experienced politics in contrasting governments, as well as absorbing the pain of marriage break-ups and deaths within her own family. Her faith, which she has spoken about often, sustains a sense of the sacredness of people and life as well as a sense of what is important and right in a society which is ethically and spiritually shifting all the time.

Both of our Elizabeths share a sense of being people who had no choice but to accept the role assigned to them. Circumstances beyond their control directed their destiny. Duty today is not perhaps a particularly attractive concept but both responded to the duty they felt to their God. At Christmas, most of us too feel the pull of some sense of duty, in some shape or form: the duty to invite and include those on the margins of our church and community to come and share in our liturgical joy and celebration; the duty we feel to invite our family members, as well as those who are lonely in the place where we live, to come and join us in some of the bountiful goodness granted to us in our own lives. Duty, although it might sound like an old-fashioned value, is no bad thing, because it reminds us that our own lives are not simply about our own gratification, that we have a responsibility to accept what God asks of us, to do what the innkeeper did and open the doors of the metaphorical stable for the sake of loving others. As Thomas Merton said, 'Duty does not have to be dull. Love can make it beautiful and fill it with life.'[2] In her 2016 Christmas Day speech, the Queen quoted Mother Teresa's mantra of making a difference to the world if 'we do small things with great love'. Indeed, this is really all we are charged to do by a missional God who understands the limitations of existence and asks us to respond in the place and situations where we find ourselves.

Elizabeth overcame what was perhaps the first spiritual duty of every follower of Jesus, and that was to embrace and carry a costly calling in courage.

Prayer ideas

- Pray for older women who are pregnant or mothers.
- Pray for those at odds with their family.
- Pray for our Queen and royal family.
- Pray for your own wider family.
- Listen to the Queen's Speech on Christmas Day.

Zechariah
Mute and miracle

———◦◦•◦◦———

I've known several men on the wrong side of 50 who have fathered children. For some this has been as a definitive choice of a second family, while others have just married later after a lengthy period of bachelordom. My own father was one such man – at the mature age of 54 he had me. Perhaps it has become more acceptable for this to happen as the idea of what constitutes a family has become much more fluid over the last few decades. The assumption that such fathers are grandparents rather than fathers might feel simultaneously amusing and strangely painful, even embarrassing to those on the receiving end of others' judgements.

Zechariah was also one such man – and even older when God granted Elizabeth the child she had yearned for all her life. It's difficult for us to imagine the shameful stigma childlessness would have caused, particularly to a couple who were considered upright and righteous. In chapter 1 verse 6 of his Gospel, Luke says they walked blamelessly in all the commandments and requirements of the Lord. Zechariah, as a priest, married the daughter of another priest, and indeed Elizabeth carried the name of Aaron's own wife, one of the original priestly tribes. But behind their backs much gossip must have flowed, for childlessness was often understood as an indicator of sin. What hidden wickedness were the couple involved in? Was Elizabeth's barrenness the result of a past estrangement from God?

In the culture of the time it would have been easy for Zechariah to quietly dispense with his wife, trade her in for a younger and more fertile model. The inability to have a child was assumed to be a female problem and was accepted grounds for divorce. But he does not do this and instead commits the whole situation to God's unfolding and greater vision, getting on with the business of devoutly serving as a member of a priestly group. The revelation that Zechariah is to become a father happens as he is performing his religious duties, ministering before the golden altar of incense in the Holy of Holies in the Temple. Each priestly group (Zechariah belonged to the order of Abijah) was asked to minister in the Temple on only two occasions during the entire year, for one week each time. In each priestly group there were approximately 1,000 priests, so this was by no means a usual occurrence for this man but an almost once-in-a-lifetime opportunity, like meeting the Queen.

So Zechariah would already have been in an awesome place, wowed by the whole occasion and his task. Along with two others he would have had to remove the still warm ashes from the previous evening's sacrifice, then reverently place a pile of new burning coals on the altar. After this, he would enter this sacred place alone and spread incense over the coals, which would exude a fragrant smoke that worshippers outside would associate with the presence of God. Like Moses and the Burning Bush, this man finds himself on deeply holy ground as an angel appears in front of him. The personal visit of such a being was a privilege afforded to very few people in the history of Israel, especially when such a divinity addresses you directly. But Zechariah is told, like Mary, not to be afraid, and the angel tells him his prayer has been answered, that Elizabeth in her dotage will become a mother and that the son born will be called John. Not only this but this boy will be significant in the plan God has for the world – he will be the herald of the dawning of a new age, the age of God's own Son.

Like a child in a sweetshop Zechariah is stunned, gobsmacked, unable to take in the information or the celestial sight in front of him. Before he has a chance to respond in an appropriate way he voices his doubts – and wouldn't we all? How can this be, my wife is old, he says. As we know, God presses the mute button on Zechariah until 'the day these things occur'. Others would have understood, as indeed he himself must have done, that this silent time was part of God's plan of contemplation and acceptance. Behind it was the sharp reminder that God is indeed a God of miracles, in charge and not to be doubted.

Silence can be a powerful and difficult challenge for us in a society which tends to over-communicate. Saturated as we are by verbal stimulation of every kind, we often lose the opportunity to listen at a level where God can be heard, in places where the holy somehow resonates. Most of us find long periods of silence difficult. A few years ago our church organized a sponsored silence to raise money for Amnesty International. A few of us just about managed 24 hours of not communicating through speech, but often I simply forgot. On reflection, this self-inflicted muteness was both a blessing and a curse. We add to our own power through what we say, particularly if we say it with passion and conviction. If we are trusted leaders then people listen to what we say, taking seriously our own beliefs and views, allowing them to dialogue with their own. On the other hand, the imposed silence was an unexpected haven, an excuse not to enter into unwanted conversations which feel tiring or pointless with the overly verbose or theologically naive.

God's act of striking such dumbness was perhaps more radical than we might understand. Radical, because Zechariah lived in a society where men's speech would have been at the forefront of importance. What women said was much less listened to or even heard, let alone taken seriously. For a man of a priestly and respected group not to be able to speak would have had serious significance. During his time of dumbness, Zechariah would have had ample time to contemplate his sudden lack of power, his reliance on God and his inability (at least verbally) to say anything. Like King Canute as he watched the force of the oncoming sea, Zechariah perhaps relaxed into a humble acceptance that he was temporarily and happily powerless against the tide of divine immensity that was God's plan.

Advent too is a season where inevitability plays a part. Sometimes, drowning in the tidal force of material buying, inevitable preparations and busyness that this season brings, we forget that Christmas is the subject of God moving miraculously and decisively among humanity. The nation of Israel had looked forward for centuries to the coming Messiah and the person who heralded him. Zechariah and Elizabeth's excitement would have built as they neared John's birth, as it does with children as 25 December approaches. Christmas is often full of surprises, and for this couple the surprise came in their child's name – John. As we saw in the previous chapter, it would have been customary for a male son to inherit the family name, but not so here. The name John means 'the Lord is gracious', and graciousness was seen in the fact that Elizabeth and Zechariah were not only given a son but told he was to be a significant person in history also.

Christmas is a time when there is an opportunity to experience and participate in such graciousness. The Christian tradition tells us that God gives according to the riches of his grace and that he does this often abundantly, going beyond what we ask for. Our job is to trust that he is the God of the miraculous, as well as to interpret where such an abundance of grace falls in our own and others' lives.

The novel *Lila* by the American novelist Marilynne Robinson is the third book of her *Gilead* trilogy. Its central theme is the unlikely marriage between the elderly John Ames and Lila, a ragtag homeless woman half his age. The story ebbs and flows between what appears to be a sometimes uncomfortable present and Lila's harsh and unpredictable past, as Ames and Lila feel their way into their marriage in a quiet and conservative town where John has been the pastor for many years. The gentle beauty of the book is filled with grace as both individuals learn to see its presence in the second chance of this perhaps miraculous opportunity as Lila discovers she is to have John's child. The acceptance and kindness of those who have long loved Ames as their priest extends as they also care gently for his broken girl of a wife, a demonstration of tangibly lived-out faithfulness.

The greatness of God's grace inspired Zechariah, when his speech returned, to proclaim his famous *Benedictus*, a canticle regularly said at the office of Morning Prayer. The song describes the miraculous happening of this story and expresses his own recognition of who God is. There is within its verses still the sentiment of his startled surprise – that he has found himself in this place, as a father in the twilight of his own life. In Robinson's book, John Ames continuously tells stories to his young wife as well as using metaphors to try to encapsulate how he feels about his own gently moving faith. He tells her the story of an unusual bird which had flown into the house. With all the doors and windows opened, the bird eventually found its way out. Ames says, 'It left a blessing in the house . . . The wildness of it. Bringing the wind inside.'[1] God brings the wind of a new era into the rabbinic tradition that Zechariah was a part of through his Spirit, leaving a man as well as a tradition transformed and steeped in grace for all time.

Prayer ideas

- Pray for those unable to have children.
- Pray for older parents.
- Pray for those praying for a miracle.
- Pray for your own priestly leaders.

Joseph
Anti-abandonment

Chicago-based installation artist Theaster Gates has, over several years, been slowly transforming the neighbourhood where he lives. Currently a professor in the Department of Visual Art and Director of Arts and Public Life at the University of Chicago, Gates came from humble beginnings. His father was a roofer and Gates describes his inheritance as being his father's tar-kettle. As an artist, he trained as a potter and made his reputation by showing and selling his pottery through a doppelganger character, a fictional Japanese fine-art ceramicist that he had entirely made up. When the art world discovered it had been duped, Gates's international reputation soared and his dubious yet entrepreneurial talents were eventually celebrated. He continued to build his reputation by collecting, exhibiting and then selling the discarded (and seemingly worthless) objects from the streets where he regularly walked. He sold these at a profit, and rather than pocketing the money he began to use his resources to buy up dilapidated buildings for the purpose of transforming them into community spaces and places to inhabit once more. His *Dorchester Projects* are well known, and Gates is the founder and director of the Rebuild Foundation, a non-profit organization committed to urban regeneration in communities which might be considered derelict, forgotten and under-resourced. In 2015 he won the acclaimed Cardiff-based Artes Mundi and promptly shared his £40,000 prize with the other nine shortlisted artists.

Through his inspiring leadership, Gates has created new spaces for his community – an abandoned bank that has become a dance studio, a library and record archive, gardening projects and a wealth of other venues where people can come together to meet, share stories and enjoy cultural life. His Soul Food Pavilion provides occasions where Sunday dinners are shared among his diverse group of friends and supporters, and cultural recipes are cooked and consumed. Guests from all backgrounds are invited to this lively communal table where issues of race, inequality and the experience of simply being a twenty-first-century human living in America are discussed. It feels, even from a distance, a deeply gospel event. Gates is clearly doing a tremendous thing in Chicago and indeed now has projects all over the world, including the music event *Sanctum* which happened in Bristol in 2015. Influenced by his own Baptist upbringing, his work and inspiration are clearly rooted in a Christian social gospel.

Gates's work is inspiring to read and experience. Commitment to transformation and a refusal to see hopelessness in situations of abandonment and blight is a powerful message anywhere. As Christians, we must be committed to cultivating something of such a culture of anti-abandonment which, translated into a theological language, means being faithful to our faith, values and buildings as well as the people we are called to love and serve. In this season of Advent, we are rightly challenged to remember those whom society pushes to one side, as well as reclaiming the members of our own family who need additional cherishing through the hospitality that we offer.

Developing an attitude of hospitality makes connections with Joseph, earthly and earthy father to Jesus, a man who refused to abandon Mary when she got herself pregnant through mysterious means. Although Joseph's official patron's day is 19 March it is important to reflect on him during this season purely because he is so much a part of the Christmas narrative. But it is only within the birth narratives of Matthew and Luke where Joseph is mentioned and after the occasion where Jesus loses himself in the crowd, only to be found wowing the teachers in the Temple, he is not mentioned again in the gospel narrative. Subsequent Christian tradition built up around the content of these Gospel accounts represents Mary as a widow. Joseph is not mentioned at the wedding in Cana nor in the Passion narrative itself. Indeed, Jesus' words to John as he hangs dying upon the cross, simply asking him to take care of his mother, would not have been necessary had his earthly father been alive. Joseph quietly disappears, it seems, after his job is done.

That said, Joseph provides an important part of the early life of Jesus and a significant character for us to reflect upon. His own attitude of anti-abandonment is exemplary. He not only stays with Mary at a time when becoming pregnant before marriage might have caused something of a stir, but travels with her to Bethlehem in uncomfortable and dangerous circumstances. The adoption of Jesus by Joseph importantly established Jesus as being descended from King David, in accordance with the prophecy that the Jewish Messiah would be 'of the house of David'.

The Gospels describe Joseph as a *tekton* – traditionally translated as 'carpenter', but the etymological root of this word is where we gather words such as 'technical' and 'technology'. It seems therefore that Joseph could just as easily have been skilled in working materials such as metal or stone. It doesn't really matter and it is possible that because of this Joseph was a trained craftsman, perhaps the proprietor of a workshop where he employed others.

Joseph's home town of Nazareth was not a place of great significance at the time of Jesus. It was situated about 65 kilometres (40 miles) from Jerusalem and near to the city of Tzippori, which was destroyed by the Romans in 4 BC. Some scholars have suggested that skilled artisans like Joseph (maybe even possibly Jesus) might have travelled daily in order to work towards the rebuilding of the city using their trained skills. But that Joseph was a practical and intelligent man appears evident, and in his later life and ministry it seems that Jesus places great emphasis on practical people of skill – he calls fishermen to join his band of close companions.

As children grow and blossom into their own unique personalities, good parents often understand that parental security and domestic stability take on a subtly new guise. The role changes from being the ever vigilant and physically attentive provider in their early years. But as children grow, being a good parent is about retreating into the background of someone's life, even if this means a lack of appreciation or recognition. For children to have clean clothes for school and sport, healthy food, lifts to friends and support with homework and through emotional crises feels of utmost importance to me as parent of two rapidly developing teens. But I recognize too that my children's emotional dependence upon me as mother is rightly diminishing as they grow into adult independence.

It appears that Joseph recognized and undertook such a role as his own God-given calling, instantaneously and willingly right from the beginning of Jesus' life. He understood, perhaps instinctively, that Mary, as mother of God's Son, was to be the person at the forefront of a bigger story of faith and history. It is assumed that Joseph acted as midwife too, in the draughty, straw-scratched stable, for no other women are mentioned as Jesus arrived in the world through ordinary flesh and fragrant incarnation. Joseph, with his practical side, would perhaps have been ideally suited for such an experience. There is a wonderful picture by Georges de la Tour, *St Joseph the Carpenter*, which shows an elderly Joseph bent double as he demonstrates the mechanism of an instrument used in carpentry to the young Jesus. The picture displays an intense intimacy between father and son, their faces lit in chiaroscuro, showing the passing on of skilled knowledge with perhaps an acceptance and irony of a future tragedy that would also end with a piece of rough wood.

To go back to our artist, Theaster Gates is also passionate about traditional craftsmanship. For him the sometimes unglamorous and old-fashioned time-consuming work that is required to make something which has a lasting legacy both of usefulness and beauty is also the stuff that provides us with a sense of purpose and dignity. In his book *Think Like an Artist*, the art critic Will Gompertz quotes Gates:

> We have to make labour more skilled and more sensitive, we have got to bring that back. We have to bring dignity back to labour. We have to assume that the entire world will not be a tech-invested world. A skilled hand will create new sectors of opportunity. Because the tech dude doesn't know how to change his plumbing anymore.[1]

With this, Gates collects the discarded material within the redundant and derelict buildings of his neighbourhood and has now created a workshop where such materials can be recreated into objects and places of new beauty. This provides jobs and brings, to people who have lost it, a sense of worth and pride. For him it is not so much about the materials themselves but more about the human capacity to shape things. He, like Joseph, sticks with a community and is committed to the people who live there: a theology of *staying* even in the middle of difficulty and depression until something gives, something is renewed and is given wings to fly.

For us, too, in a land far away from Chicago and Nazareth, there is a choice about how we use the resources (individual and corporate) and talents we have, as well as a choice about how we commit to the place where we live and to others. We have a choice about how we mould and shape our own attitudes and how we spend our time – selfishly, for our own sphere and gain, or for the community in which we are a part. Any contribution we can offer is to give ourselves in service and love to God.

I imagine Joseph was steadfast, solid as a personality, someone practical, unflappable in a crisis, not overly verbose, a person who got on with the job in hand and who lived out values of faithfulness and anti-abandonment. More significantly, he was a man who understood the immensity of the part he was to play in God's plan and knew his own place within it. His humility, often depicted as 'Joseph the Worker', is divinely appropriate. Joseph surely was a man of dignity – a man who knew his craft and used it in refusing to abandon those God had put in his care. Oswald Chambers, an English spiritual writer of the late nineteenth century, says this: 'The one mark of a saint is the moral originality which springs from abandonment to Jesus Christ' – perhaps the only appropriate abandonment is to leave behind our individual desires to work for a larger vision of love, as seen in the lives of both Theaster Gates and St Joseph himself.[2]

Prayer ideas

- Pray for all parents who struggle through social reputation and poverty.
- Pray for those working in social regeneration.
- Pray for community artists who create new spaces of beauty and refreshment.
- Pray for those seeking to regenerate skilled crafts that have been lost.
- Pray for those whose name is Joseph.

The Wise Men
Recognizing God

The figures of the three Wise Men or Magi are perhaps some of the most mysterious in the New Testament. I have visions of quasi-magicians in exotic robes arguing over the stars in rooms piled to the ceiling with alchemy manuals and swirling potions which Harry Potter himself might have been proud of. But we can be forgiven for such creative licence because the English word 'magician' comes from the same root as 'Magi'. Historical research tells us that the Magi were not the Derren Browns of today but men of noble birth, educated and expert in astrology and familiar with Hebrew Scriptures. They were most probably wealthy, and people of wisdom and influence. Who else would bring gifts of careful consideration and financial cost? Some scholars believe the men were priests or seers from the Zoroastrian religion.

When we look at the story in the cold light of day it feels more than slightly fantastical in terms of probability. Why would three men (the text does not tell us of their relationship and whether they knew each other before travel) undertake such a risky and uncomfortable journey to visit a poor unknown child? Their reasons were a combination of factors. They had studied the Scriptures and alighted on a verse in Micah which they found particularly significant: 'But you, O Bethlehem of Ephrathah, who are one of the little clans of Judah, from you shall come forth for me one who is to rule in Israel, whose origin is from of old, from ancient days' (Micah 5.2). They probably also understood the prophecy which appears in chapter 9 of the book of Daniel, concerning a propitious time when the Messiah was meant to be returning. All of this colliding with the appearance of an especially bright star in a particularly significant place in the night sky meant auspiciousness, which resulted in the obedient undertaking of a journey. Like Abraham before them, these Magi knew not at first where they were to go but merely set out in courage and faith, following the guiding star which led them on their way.

We all know the outcome of this journey – perhaps one which transformed their lives. The strange juxtaposition of men in luxuriant robes trailing their finery through the mess and muck of a straw-filled stable is one which has been well documented. Traditionally the presence of the Wise Men at the birth scene has symbolized the relevance and inclusion of all peoples to hear and absorb the person and message of Christ. The whole world is symbolized in this humble stable – the local (in the shepherds), the international (in the Wise Men) and indeed the inclusion of the whole of the created order in the presence of the animals which surround the baby to give him warmth.

Essentially the Magi attempted something notoriously problematic by recognizing the action and the asking of God in their lives. Most importantly they decisively acted upon their understood knowledge. I spend my current working life listening to a whole variety of seemingly crazy and often improbable stories of where and how others believe they have heard God calling them into the ordained ministry. Over the last few years I have heard many stories of conversion. One candidate changed from atheism to belief through the scientific study of the human brain; his argument – how could there be something so complex without a Creator? Other callings originate from bizarre dreams and visions – burning crosses held high and an image of a church with no walls where people come and go freely to worship a God who is living and meaningful. As with the Wise Men, a sound recognition of God's presence in any life is often a multiple experience – it is a proper reading of and reflection on the biblical text (their reading of the Hebrew Scriptures) with a connection to and impact on a present life in the now (the viewing of the star).

But for many, recognizing, listening to and hearing God in any life is hard and needs teaching 'how to' in terms of discernment and prayer. Is hearing God in our lives the taking seriously of the things we find uncomfortable about contemporary life, the things which do not sit comfortably with how society is going? Is recognizing God that yearning to do something for others; is it having a heart for a particular group of people or cause and then acting on it? To recognize where God is will never hold complete certainty for any of us, but there can be no doubt that many people are emotionally and intellectually convinced that they have discerned the voice or presence of God in their lives. Sometimes this is taught, but often not – often it is the metaphorical sweeping of us off our unexceptional feet which has subsequent seismic spiritual consequences. And often the beginning of our own journey of recognition is one which others in the Bible have begun tentatively and learned to do better. The Magi, for example, stepped out in faith, recognizing the time was right to follow the star to the important king. Mary Magdalen needed a little help in recognizing the resurrected Christ in the Garden of Gethsemane, and the disciples on the road to Emmaus had to spend quite a lot of time walking and talking before they knew who the inscrutable stranger who had joined them actually was.

In his recent book *Amazing Love,* Andrew Davison cites John Calvin's idea that God takes into account our misted eyes, saying that

> God accommodates divine truth to human communication, using forms and figures that speak to us. Revelation unfolds in time and after revelation is complete, the task of unfolding the meaning of such revelation then becomes central to the life of the Church.[1]

The point is that we live a veiled life. There are archetypical 'thin' spaces and places, maybe even personality types who have more chance to recognize, absorb, 'catch' something of the divine life. We are all also influenced by our past experiences and prejudices. Yet most people can cite places, times and seasons where they have felt particularly tuned in, spiritually acute and astute to God's presence with them in some shape or form. Thomas Merton said, 'God is hidden within me. I find him by hiding in the silence in which he is concealed.'[2] Advent means just this – God 'with us' – and is a season where we should remind ourselves not only that he is indeed with us at every moment, minute, hour, but that Advent calls Christian people to help those who seek to recognize the presence of God in their own lives too.

This feels to me like an underestimated missional ministry for the Church of today. We are often not teaching others new to faith how to do this simple thing. And so often it is simply a fitting together of a numinous experience someone has already had with an explanation that here, here is where God is.

Embedded in the story of the Wise Men are the crucial qualities needed for such recognition and subsequent potential conversion to follow. First, there was clearly effort involved in their decision to begin the journey. We have an image of them poring over the verses in the Scriptures, studying the pathway of the stars, weighing things up, maybe arguing and finally stepping out in courage. Seeing and hearing the presence and action of God takes effort, as any serious grappling and practice of faith does. Second, even if they did not previously know one another they must have established some kind of relationship in order to travel together. God with us is always relational and about learning to see the presence of God within others. Douglas Rhymes says:

> To have a prayerful approach to people is to have eyes to see, a mind intent upon seeing, a heart hopeful of seeing the image of God in each person I meet, to see them in themselves and in God.[3]

This was indeed the ministry of Jesus, to enable those he encountered to see who they really were – from Simon the Pharisee to the several blind people he physically cured and spiritually enabled to understand the nature of the kingdom.

Recognizing God is also about humility – a quality the Magi must have had. Why else would three men of traditional wealth and status bow down before a small impoverished child with no previous noble history? To recognize God, as St Francis says, we must, 'Start by doing what is necessary, then do what is possible, and suddenly you are doing the impossible.' Finding faith often comes with willpower to 'just do it'; then comes the faithful practice of it, and slowly we are transformed. Jesus challenges us to live in our earthly and earthy reality and to learn to perceive the depth dimensions of all our experiences which point to God.

Prayer ideas

- Pray for those who want to have faith but struggle to find it.
- Pray for those at the beginning of their faith journey, particularly those you know.
- Pray for those who travel in dangerous places.
- Pray for your church community to be a rich diversity of all sections of the community.

Saintly shepherds
Sacred staying

Stereotypes need to be shattered. And my own just have been, after reading James Rebanks's extraordinarily beautiful and illuminating account of living a shepherd's life in the land of the Lake District. This evocative book has made me realize that I have been carrying around for years, albeit subconsciously, the image of the shepherd as thick and rough-shod yokel. As I read through its pages I sensed my embedded prejudices slipping away over a precipice of past and over-simplified judgements.

Our calling as Christian people is to look continually for the links between the person who is God and the stuff which is our life, and the life of a twentieth-century shepherd has much to say to those of us who are trying to follow Jesus, those of us who yearn to feel God's presence. There is the obvious stuff – shepherds are resilient, faithful, committed to the lands which remain so integral to their way of life. Rebanks's book – *The Shepherd's Life* – has become a national phenomenon and he enjoys a following on Twitter of more than 30,000. What is it about his account which has caught the public imagination so much? Perhaps it is a sensed intuition that such a life indeed speaks of the power of the ordinary as well as the mystery of the divine.

The author describes a mixture of inherited and inherent knowledge of a species and land which is hugely complex. Good shepherds need to know their sheep – when they are lambing and whether they will survive when they are sick. They need to learn a sense of which sheep are of good stock for breeding, for the continuation of the flock, and how to 'heft' – that is, to establish an animal in the land on which it roams so that it feels instinctually that this is its place, the land where it resides, the land which is home. Shepherds need to know how to negotiate hard financial deals and understand the interrelationships of different farmers, lands and herds. Such expertise is built up not from books but from handed-down experience. Good shepherds need to be resilient, and Rebanks recounts the tragedy of the foot and mouth epidemic in 2001 which wiped out so many flocks and was largely misunderstood by a government in a capital far away. Shepherds take as normal the hard graft of the accepted daily faithfulness so necessary to care for the sheep – in spring making sure lambs are connected with their mothers and protected from the cold and predators, and in winter making sure sheep deep in snowdrifts have access to enough food. Being a shepherd is no picnic, and there is much nonsensical romance around the image of shepherds in literature as well as from the Christmas story. The average wage of a shepherd is £8,500 per annum so most today have to supplement this income through other means. To be a shepherd today, as well as 2,000 years ago, requires qualities of instinctual loyalty, earthed practicality, compassion, respect for nature and emotional and physical robustness.

I have always wondered why some of the first people God chose to reveal himself to were shepherds. The fact that these men were local and the Wise Men came from lands far away has been much pondered on, a metaphor for God's coming to the whole of the world in all its glorious diversity. But it is more than this. Throughout his book, Rebanks describes a sense of loyalty to *place*, a feeling he has had all his life. This was the reason he didn't want to 'get on' at school, as well as the reason he felt deeply alien in the academic environment of Oxford when he eventually went to study there. He describes the fact that the shepherd's life was and is the *only* life he ever really wanted to live: 'men and women who were good shepherds were held in the highest esteem, regardless of being to modern eyes "just employees". To be a shepherd was to stand as tall as any man.'[1]

Education today is perhaps obsessed with 'getting on and getting out' – we have to push ourselves and our children, and certainly where I grew up, the idea of moving swiftly away from a county that seemed to be at the end of the world (Cornwall) took on a kind of desperate urgency. The idea of *staying* there out of a love and loyalty for the geographical place would have felt frankly ludicrous. I wanted to go somewhere far more exciting than a land of grey pebbledash housing and salty sea. Rebanks's yearning to stay, to remain because of a sense of deeply felt love for land and animals, is countercultural but one also which connects strongly and inevitably with the Incarnation – a theological principle firmly embedded within the seasons of Advent and Christmas. The Christ-event is to be discovered in every place in this world, in every person, object, creature, in some sense. Rebanks speaks with poignant beauty about the resistance to leaving behind a valuable and traditional way of life which is fast disappearing and about a deepening of what is already there. His book is also about the determined refusal to lose a tradition and profession which contains some of the depths of what it means to live a human and holy life.

The saints described in this book, like the shepherds, are often associated with a specific place where their lives following God are lived out and witnessed by others. Over the years their reputation has grown, but for many this has happened posthumously. There is something about holiness that is similarly and inevitably about anonymity. The life of the shepherds in Rebanks's account is contrasted sharply with the parallel universe of tourism, for which the Lakes are also so well known and loved. Reading one of Wainwright's guides prompted him to say:

> So I was looking down at the landscape farmed by my father's friends and cross checking it against the guide. It struck me powerfully that there was scarcely a trace of any of the things we cared about in what Wainwright had written. Apart from the odd dot on the map for a farm or a wall, nothing from our world appeared in those pages. I wondered whether the walkers on the mountain saw the working side of that landscape, and whether it mattered. In my bones I felt it did matter. That seeing, understanding and respecting people in their own landscape is crucial to their culture and ways of life being valued and sustained. What you don't see you don't care about.[2]

Rebanks also describes the perception that the life of a shepherd is the life of a nobody, of someone considered irrelevant, stupid and invisible. But God picked the biblical shepherds as the chosen and privileged people to be the first witnesses to the birth of Christ because this is a turning upside-down of worldly values, perhaps because within their humanity they contained and existentially lived out the qualities needed to be a follower of Jesus – resilience, faithfulness, a love and respect of the created world, common sense and a natural sense of the transcendent. The writer himself says it feels the most natural thing to go to church on Christmas Eve. Shepherds are 'big picture' people, human beings who have a community-based relationship with one another and the emerald land on which they walk, continuously dealing with the essential and important things of human existence – life, death, love and loyalty. They understand what it means to be and feel alive through how they care, what they witness and in the gritty determination they model.

> There is the thrill in the timelessness up there. I have always liked the feeling of carrying something bigger than me, something that stretched back through other hands and other eyes into the depths of time. To work there is a humbling thing, the opposite of conquering a mountain, if you like; it liberates you from any illusion of self-importance.[3]

The shepherds at the time of Jesus were far from random guests at his birth. They were carefully chosen people, chosen for the qualities they distinctively and instinctively possessed which are the qualities of the saints, characteristics necessary for and connected to the life lived in faithfulness, deep love and clear-sightedness. God chose to send his heavenly hosts to first reveal their astonishing message in a place of unremarkable non-identity – a field just north of the stable at the back of an overcrowded inn in the little town of Bethlehem. On Christmas Eve God comes to earth as lover and child, and

> every ordinary, created thing has become transparent with his glory. There is gold in the straw and myrrh in the dung on the floor . . . For tonight let us revel in the light of that star beneath which the ordinary becomes holy and the holy ordinary, beneath which it becomes exceedingly clear that there is nothing more we must do or be to be loved by God.[4]

Through the shepherds, indeed *the* Good Shepherd, God says, 'I am here, right here, stay in this land. I am real and I am relevant and you – yes, you, simple and skilled shepherd – have much to say to the world.'

Prayer ideas

- Pray for shepherds everywhere.
- Pray for those who farm the land, particularly food producers in this country.
- Pray for those struggling to survive financially in rural communities.
- Pray for those involved in preserving disappearing traditions and skills.

The innkeeper
Inn-convenient hospitality

The doorbell rings. It's 6.00 p.m. and I have three saucepans sizzling on the stove. I go to the door and my heart sinks – it's another charity worker. But on this occasion I push aside those unholy thoughts of inconvenience and irritation and smile at the young woman before me who is trying to raise money for a small charity based in India. I talk to her, human being to human being, she laughs at my comical apron and I invite her in. She tells me about her charity and asks me about my life. I tell her that only this morning in my prayers I felt a nudge to review my charitable giving and prayed that an opportunity would naturally arise to know which one to choose. Having told me she is a Buddhist her face displays astonishment but also a mysterious recognition at the apparent coincidence. I agree to give the charity a regular donation, she takes a selfie with me, we laugh and she goes on her way. I feel strangely warmed, as John Wesley might have said, touched by a life lived for others (she is not paid to do this work), in the knowledge I have responded in a way appropriate to my clerical office and Christian faith.

Henri Nouwen once commented that the interruptions he experienced during his working day were actually more his 'work' than the perceived and organized tasks and projects in his diary. It's a profound observation but so hard to live out. I admit to liking my own time compartmentalized, my life organized, and when something, often time-consuming, gets in the way, I am reminded that patience is not always my strongest virtue.

Perhaps this is how the innkeeper, running a local hostelry already stuffed full of people who had arrived in town for the census, actually felt. The text tells us there was no room anywhere and we can imagine him harassed by the demands of his staff and guests. I have often reflected on the job of pub landlord, making connections with the role of a priest. Both priest and landlord are required to be people of hospitality and welcome, with the ability to be able to talk naturally to a wide variety of individuals. On the other hand, they also need to know when someone wants to 'just be', staring into a pint sitting at the bar or sitting alone at the back of church. Both involve physical stamina with lots to juggle and late nights, with resilience and strong organization being vital characteristics of living on the job and 'in the role'.

So we can imagine the scene, the innkeeper frantically running around, pouring drinks, organizing food, arranging accommodation, and then this little family, bedraggled from a long and tiring journey, rock up on the doorstep. The man looks tired and anxious – his wife is about to have a baby. Please, they beg, is there really nothing you can do? We know the rest of the story – the stable, the back room with the beasts, is their only option. Joseph says 'yes'– he is desperate for any kind of roof over their heads.

The point is that the activity of God cannot often be controlled or regulated. God asks things of us at the most inconvenient of times. In my prayers I ask that when there is to be change all will flow and fit together and all will be well. No doubt it will and I believe that the Almighty does have our best interests at heart, but this isn't always how things feel. The innkeeper was asked to exercise a ministry of hospitality at the worst time it could possibly have been for him – when he was harassed and far from collected. But in the end he offered it, even if this was a little grudgingly.

The ministry of hospitality is one which every Christian can put in place in some capacity. Hospitality is deeply embedded in the gospel narrative and is at the very heart of the story of Mary herself, who uses her own body to welcome and nurture Jesus. When church communities exercise a genuine and thought-through welcome it is often powerful enough for strangers to want to remain. But it is again easy to welcome when we feel prepared – the meal is cooked, the table set, the house ordered, the beds made. What about the person arriving on the doorstep in floods of tears when we are in the middle of the only time we have to write our sermon or when we have others to manage during a contentious meeting? What about the time I collapse through the door after a hectic and intense day at work and there are 15 school bags in the hallway belonging to friends of my intensely sociably teenage daughter?

We never know when we will need the kindness of others. Jesus enjoyed the hospitality of friends like Martha and Mary but also of strangers like Zacchaeus. He himself carried a kind of 'attitude of hospitality' wrapped around his own transient ministry. People felt able to come to him with their questions and woes, instinctively trusting he would be compassionate and welcoming to them, perhaps especially those whom society pushed to the edges.

For me, exercising hospitality is the delight of faith and ministry: not quite knowing when we are going to be asked next to be hospitable, to provide a hot drink, to listen to a lonely person, to provide a safe space for a young person who does not enjoy a stable home. The other thing about hospitality is that it does not have to be made up of grandiose or sanctimonious gestures – it just needs to be willing and ordinary. Here is a reflection I have shared several times about my own current hospitality to the many teenagers who use our large rectory as unofficial youth club:

At the end of last year, my daughter Eve asked me the question I had been dreading. 'Mum, can I have a party for my 15th birthday?' She had had one the previous year – but of course then she had been a year younger. Because we had survived the previous year's event I found myself agreeing, in consultation with my husband. However, as our house is a rectory we stipulated absolutely no alcohol, either purchased by us or brought in by them.

The day came – actually a Friday, officially our day off. Eve had invited 'no more than 35, Mum' and of course I was placated by her saying that most of these kids were known to us. But as the evening approached my sense of dread and foreboding increased. Eve had emphasized that at the first sight of any gate-crashers or if things got out of hand she would come and get us (we were going to be barricaded in our large front room with back-up friend and the cat). 'And if anyone vomits, the party's over,' I said.

We prepared the downstairs part of our house by removing breakables and rugs (we have mostly laminate flooring in our large hall, very large kitchen, even larger conservatory and small TV room) and shut ourselves away. The party actually kicked off around 6.45 p.m. (it was meant to be 7.00 p.m.).

I survived the next four and a half hours by playing board games, drinking strong coffee and being reassured by my very calm husband and friend. But pumping music and very loud boisterous lads yelling, 'It's time for a football chant!' on several occasions didn't help. At one point our then 12-year-old son texted my husband, saying, 'Dad, they're everywhere. I'm not coming down!' Although we did emerge at various points – my husband to talk nicely with the group of ten older gate-crashers and to cast a parental eye around – I am happy to say we survived, although at 11.15 p.m. when everyone was out of the house the downstairs did look like a war zone. I found bottles (smuggled in secretly) in places I never knew existed in our home, and in one room it looked as though there had been a soft fall of freshly crushed Pringles absolutely everywhere. But after several bin bags of empty and unsurprising bottle collections and several mops of the floor, I stood and drank the remainder of our Christmas port and smoked a cigarette I only ever smoke on occasions of extreme stress or relief.

The party was a success and I am pleased. I was also hugely touched by the genuine 'thank yous' I received from these young folk, who don't have many places to do this kind of thing: 'Thank you for letting us use your house,' and lots of hugs. The thing is, it's actually wonderful – I love these young people, many from broken homes, but all vulnerable and fragile and about to launch themselves into the world. My heart goes out to them just as Jesus' did when he saw the hungry crowd who had faithfully listened to his teaching for many a long hour.

This is implemented, ordinary hospitality, and genuine because it cost me something in time, energy, money and anxiety. Hospitality is often about ourselves and others crossing a threshold. God did this through the Incarnation, decisively initiating an encounter with the world through our beautiful and fragile humanity. The act of birth itself crosses a threshold from incubation to a life which cries and pulsates, laughs and experiences. When we welcome others they often step through the church door or our own front door. Threshold symbolizes the beginning of a new state of being or consciousness, a new experience or encounter. How we treat others matters and is noticed and can have serious impact, both positively or negatively.

The innkeeper is a rebel within a book about saints, for of course he is far from a recognized holy person, either in December's lectionary or as a particularly honourable character within the Christmas story. But perhaps he can represent those unsung heroes who offer hospitality to others, consciously or inadvertently, in our churches and communities, and as they do so enable God's own welcome to be tangibly experienced by all who receive it.

Prayer ideas

- Pray for a genuine spirit of hospitality in our church communities.
- Pray to demonstrate hospitality in new and creative ways.
- Pray for those who offer a special ministry in this way.
- Pray for those who do not feel welcome within their families and communities.

Stephen

We are connected

Boxing Day in my household is permeated by a vague sense of relief – the Christmas services are over for another year, this is the day when relatives staying over Christmas take their leave, then the rest of the day can be spent relaxing over copious glasses of alcohol and watching seasonal detective dramas. The only creative energy required is thinking up a leftover turkey recipe.

Yet 26 December is a poignant and significant day in the Anglican calendar, the day when now only the most faithful of Anglo-Catholic churches might remember the Church's deacon and first martyr, Stephen. Reading his story – the lengthy speech in Acts 7 – feels like eating a lemon after the complacency of a day of festivities. His eloquent and emotional speech before the Sanhedrin once more sharpens our own awareness of the costliness of Christian witness. We are awake again as Stephen shows us that there is no respite on our journey towards the holy, his witness a tangible reminder of the life of Christ himself. Robert Atwell, the Bishop of Exeter, interprets Luke's description of Stephen as bearing direct parallels to the person of Christ. Stephen's actions mirror Jesus' own – both are filled with the Holy Spirit, Stephen sees the Son of God at the right hand of God as was Jesus' own promise of himself, Stephen 'commends his own spirit' to God, just as Jesus did, and Stephen kneels, as Jesus did at his moment of anguish in Gethsemane, as well as asking for forgiveness and mercy from those persecuting him.[1] The fact that we remember his story the day after Jesus' birth sends out the message that every Christian person is called in some way to embody the Spirit of Christ and to witness to his love.

Stephen was one of seven deacons appointed by the apostles to distribute food and charitable aid to poorer members of the community. There was mounting dissatisfaction among the Greek-speaking Jews that their widows were being slighted in preference for Hebraic women in the distribution of alms from communal funds. Acts 6 mentions that Stephen performed miracles among the people, and it seems that he was teaching in many of the local synagogues. Opposition and irritation towards him was building and members of the conservative religious establishment had previously been challenging his teachings. But Stephen proved himself to be a talented and convincing orator; his sweep of the history of Israel in Acts 7 culminates in the belief that God does not reside solely in one building, in this case the Temple, an idea which would have been highly offensive to traditional Jews. Included in his recounting is the secondary theme of Israel's disobedience to God. Despite his best efforts to show that Jesus came not to destroy the law of Moses but to fulfil it, his argument falls on deaf ears. Calling his listeners 'stiff-necked' people doesn't help and only gives them every excuse to dispose of this outspoken orator in a way fitting for all who are accused of blasphemy. These men are stiff-necked because they refuse to recognize the presence and action of the Holy Spirit, just as their ancestors did. The faithful Jews hearing his impassioned speech are deaf to everything but unconventionality and untrue faith. Stephen is taken out of the city and stoned, thus becoming the Church's first martyr.

A detail which seems small as we read the text and yet is hugely significant is that this incident is observed by the future St Paul. At this point in his life he is still Saul, a faithful and traditional Jew who, we are told, approved of Stephen's murder. But here is the redemption, because we understand the big picture as twenty-first-century followers. We know what happens next – that sooner or later Saul is transformed, temporarily blinded; he has a direct experience of Christ and literally 'sees the light' a few chapters later. This continues to be one of the most powerful conversion experiences in the Bible, primarily because it gives breathing space for even the most heinous of oppressors to have their dark lives flooded with new light. For those of us who have attempted to live a Christian life for many years, we perhaps take for granted the dramatic power of this light. I write this a few days before the clocks go back, when many of us will leave for work as well as return from it in darkness.

Just as Stephen links the present action of God with the past faithfulness of divine life, the figure of Saul/Paul is linked through the witness of Stephen. Our life lived with God connects us always to those who have gone before us. It is difficult sometimes for us to understand the workings of the world; we strain to extract a sense of divine justice from the lives of those who suffer terribly and undeservedly in this world. We are called to be people of hope, and we believe and have biblical evidence that God can break into lives of apparent immovability and stubbornness and that these, in their turn, can be instrumental in someone else's future faith. My own prayers often incorporate a yearning for someone somewhere to be transformed radically through God's love and light; for someone somewhere to turn away from a doctrine of hate and wrongful indoctrination and be electrified, as Paul himself was, with divine light. Here we have the evidence – Saul was brought literally to his knees, and entered a period of darkness as he moved into a new repentance and life lived in Christ.

Christmas is often a time when we get together with those we do not see much, friends and relatives we are connected with yet who are dispersed. Likewise, we may bump into others in church whom we have not seen for years. Recently a couple visited my church; he had been the previous vicar of my mother-in-law's church many miles away, and they were on holiday. I didn't recognize them until they came and introduced themselves after the service. We never know who will wash up in our lives after years of losing touch. The story and witness of Stephen goes further than this, for it proves there is a profound redemption made possible through the workings of God's powerful Spirit. Paul at the time looked on, experiencing an ugly spectacle of the killing of an innocent and God-focused man. He was not to know that through Stephen's own prayer his own life would be radically changed.

The true story of Eric Lomax, a British soldier who was captured and tortured by the Japanese in Singapore, has been well documented in both writing and the recent film *The Railway Man*. Forced to work on the Thai–Burma railway during the Second World War, Lomax was also tortured by the military secret police for making an improvised radio receiver. The physical and psychological abuse he endured inevitably had profound consequences, especially as Lomax's actual intention had been purely innocent. Rather than producing the radio to communicate with British forces elsewhere, his actual aim had been to simply create some form of entertainment to boost the morale of fellow prisoners.

After years of traumatic memory, Lomax decided to return to the Far East to attempt to find the officer responsible for the damage and pain he had suffered. With the help of his wife and a friend, Lomax tracked down Takashi Nagase to attempt to let go of a lifetime of bitterness and hate. After meeting Nagase and learning that over the years he had made more than 60 missions of atonement to the River Kwai, had become a devout Buddhist and had financed a Buddhist peace temple, Lomax realized this man was serious about repenting of his former deeds. In his memoir, Lomax writes:

> Meeting Nagase has turned him from a hated enemy, with whom friendship would have been unthinkable, into a blood brother. If I'd never been able to put a name to the face of one of the men who had harmed me, and never discovered that behind that face there was also a damaged life, the nightmares would always have come from a past without meaning.[2]

Paul did not have the luxury of meeting one of those he indirectly had a hand in killing, for Stephen's life ended on the tragic day of his stoning. Yet the redemption and responsibility lies in the importance of the contribution that Stephen made to enable Paul to become more fully alive, pulled from a deadening violence into which he had been locked. None of us ever knows the potential contribution we make to others' lives through our own witness, faithfulness and love. Mary Grey, in her book *The Wisdom of Fools*, puts it like this:

> This is why political and social transformation must first be on the level of our philosophical consciences and symbolic order. Invitations to connect, reconnect, or build relationships around the notion of mutuality will make no difference until the all-pervasiveness of the notion of separation – even within theology itself – is recognized, together with the difficulties of moving away from this to restructure on the basis of connection: *to discover 'the connected self' in a connected world.*[3]

Prayer ideas

- Pray for victims of torture and those who abuse others.
- Pray for those who struggle with pain-filled memories.
- Pray for those recently converted – that their stories may be encouraging and hope-filled.
- Pray for the friends and families of those who have been killed and those who have 'disappeared'.

John the Apostle and Evangelist
I am with you

———◄•►———

I like going to the cinema on my own sometimes because if I need to cry then it's not embarrassing. But I also go alone because as a happily married wife and mother it's good to be reminded of what it feels like to have to do things solo. Times like this take me back to the loneliness as well as the strange refreshment of times when I have been single. But equally I love going with friends, long-term friends, parish friends, family members. We remember these 'occasions' when we look back through our lives.

I went to see the brilliant film *I, Daniel Blake* towards the end of 2016. The film is set in present-day Newcastle-upon-Tyne and centres on a man who has been laid off work because of a heart attack. Probably in his late 50s or early 60s, a practical man and skilled carpenter, Daniel (now a widower) struggles with the intricacies and frustrations of the benefits system. The film comically and tragically highlights the fact that a lack of computer skills can have serious detrimental effects on a person's well-being because, these days, everything is dealt with and processed online. Because of his inability to crack this system, Daniel's journey is a downward spiral into frightening and rapid poverty. The film also movingly charts his unusual friendship with Katie, a single mum, and Daniel's growing support of her, herself vulnerable and at the mercy of the benefits system. Katie is so poor she resorts to stealing sanitary products from her local corner shop, as well as working as an escort girl.

In a nutshell, the film is a succinct statement about the importance and preciousness of every human person. Ironically, the systems and bureaucracies which aim to help us often end up dehumanizing people instead, depersonalizing individuality and transforming us as named individuals with needs into anonymous 'clients, service users and National Insurance numbers'. Daniel's swansong is his defiant writing of his own name as a statement of his personhood across the outside of the Job Centre among the cheers of the watching crowd who understand his frustrations, probably because of their own experiences. It's a triumphant (but sad) film about our individual dignity before God, and has the theme of how important this is to us in a myriad ways. It is also about the mysterious way that the most unlikely human beings can form strong and staunch bonds of genuine friendship.

As the year rolls to an end Advent seems distant, and as we begin to contemplate putting the decorations back in the loft we remember John the Apostle and Evangelist, a man who provided an unwavering presence as friendship to Jesus himself. John is the man whose lyrical language mesmerizes listeners every Christmas with words of mysterious beauty from chapter 1 of his Gospel. John is also reputedly the disciple 'whom Jesus loved'; he was one of the sons of Zebedee and he accompanied Jesus throughout his ministry, inhabiting his life as much as his own. John walked up the mountain where Jesus was transfigured, he sat beside him at the Last Supper, he waited nervously in the Garden of Gethsemane, was there with the women at the foot of the cross waiting for the cruel agony of crucifixion to be over and was there as a witness of the resurrection, where he 'saw and believed'.

If there is anything which keeps us going in life it is the presence and faithfulness of our friends, those who inhabit our lives to such an extent that they share the genuine celebrations as well as the extended tragedies. And maybe this living of a parallel life with Jesus was what enabled John to become such a powerful evangelist, to tell his own story of God, having lived it with such immediacy. There aren't many human lives that cannot recollect some memory of the past faithfulness of a friend. I still remember the times when one friend or another listened to my endless retelling and pondering about the end of a failed relationship as my heart slowly healed, or offered a gentle and non-judgemental presence as I recounted another disappointment or continuous anxiety. Good friendship tends not to preach or offer advice; it simply waits bravely within the darkness, offering a hand to hold with an understanding that there are no easy answers in the un-resolution of life. We are not told why Jesus especially loved John, but maybe, like so many friendships, it was because he was just this – the right presence, simply someone good to be with.

There is so much in the season of Advent and Christmas which is about keeping faithful. We sing 'O come, all ye faithful', and it is a good thing that coming to church is still understood as part of a potential 'Christmas experience'. The famous canticle the *Magnificat* is crammed with imagery of God's faithfulness, a theme which is irretrievably threaded through the biblical text like writing through a stick of rock. In a reflection given on Good Friday in 1979, Archbishop Oscar Romero emphasized to those listening that it is often when God seems most absent that he is closest to us; that it is at times like this that *we* are called to keep faithful to Christ, to continue to pray even when we do not feel like it because life has dealt us a hard blow. He quoted Jesus' words shouted in despair from the cross, and commented:

> When are we going to understand that God is not only a God who gives happiness but that he tests our faithfulness in moments of affliction? It is then that prayer and religion have most merit; when one is faithful despite not feeling the Lord's presence. Let us learn from that cry of Christ that God is always our Father and never forsakes us, and that we are closer to him than we think.[1]

To return to Mary, whom we reflected on right at the beginning of this season, this was her experience too. As we contemplate our New Year diets and hoover up the pine needles from the Christmas tree, we too can continue something of John's own witness of faithfulness into the New Year. To stay with God, and to stay with God through our experience of friendship with others, is to live and offer a powerful ministry. In *I, Daniel Blake* there is an incredibly moving scene when Daniel and Katie visit a food bank together, for they are both desperate. Katie is so hungry she opens a can of cold baked beans and starts shovelling them into her mouth but then feels devastated at her desperate state and bursts into tears. The kindness and reassurance of Daniel, who is *with* her in this God-given place, as well as of the staff (the church volunteers who actually run the food bank for real) and their lack of judgement, had me in tears. But this is something we can all do as followers of a God who challenges us to inhabit the shoes of others, to feel as they do the holes in their humanity and to fill them with kindness.

To offer friendship like this is something we can all do as we think about our New Year resolutions. One resolution we can all have is to model the qualities which John possessed – not only to be a faithful friend to Christ himself but to possess such faith in the power of God through it all. Mary had this in bucketloads – her song, the *Magnificat*, is evidence of a belief in God's greatness of divine happenings which had not even occurred yet.

> Where are these words coming from? She is no politician, no revolutionary; she simply wants to sing a happy song, but all of a sudden, she has become an articulate radical, an astonished prophet singing about a world in which the last have become first and the first last. What is more, her song puts it all in the past tense, as if the hungry have *already* been fed, the rich *already* freed from their inordinate possessions. How can that be? Her baby is no bigger than a thumbnail, but already she is reciting his accomplishments as if they were history. Her faith is in the things not seen, faith that comes to her from outside herself, and that is why we call her blessed.[2]

To stay with someone or something, to stay somewhere if we need to, is to be faithful and steadfast, which remains countercultural in our easily dispensable and throw-away Western world. This remains the radical witness of John the Apostle, as well as the radical message of Advent and Christmas and the hope faith has for the world.

Prayer ideas

- Pray for your own faith and faithfulness to others to increase if necessary.
- Pray for your own friends.
- Pray for more faithfulness in relationships.
- Pray for yourself as you move closer to the person God wants you to be this coming year.

Holy Innocents
Lives never forgotten

It is a sobering thing to remember the day when hundreds of children were needlessly and cruelly killed. On 28 December every year we are challenged to remember the Holy Innocents – the male children under two years of age who were sought out and obliterated by King Herod in the obsessional search to find his rival, Jesus. The children are described as 'innocent', as if somehow if they were guilty we might feel better about it. But the point is children are always innocent in this sense. It feels especially poignant when evil hits them because they inhabit bodies, minds, hearts not yet fully formed; there is something especially sacred about their vulnerable humanity in the form of buds rather than fully unfurled flowers.

I remember being chilled to the core one muggy day in the tropical heat of Cambodia. Visiting the site of the infamous Killing Fields we saw first hand the trenches where thousands of ordinary men and women were savagely exterminated by the Khmer Rouge. But when we arrived at the tree against which guards had smashed the heads of babies I began to feel physically sick. This happened in my own lifetime and it is a natural existential question to ask, 'Why not my children?' It is just a twist of fate that they were born and raised in a country safe and away from a regime of terror such as this.

As a mother (but perhaps this doesn't make any difference at all?) I find cruelty to children a particularly horrendous as well as genuinely confusing concept to contemplate. Jim Thompson, in his book *Stepney Calling: Thoughts for our day*, reminds us that we do not have to go far to explore the reality and possibility of evil, for it 'should be studied in the battlefield of our own mind. If we find it there, we can be sure that in the affairs of society, in the great affairs of the nations, it will be rampant.'[1] Take this and impact it with an atheistic and ideological hegemony such as extreme Communism, then add years of indoctrination and maybe it is possible to arrive at a place where reasonable people can explain why such an atrocity could happen. But there is still a part of us that must ask, 'How can a human being become so steeped in evil as to be able to wrench a child from its mother and smash its skull on a tree trunk? How can another human being see that as acceptable? How can someone see amputating the hands of children, as Joseph Kony did in Uganda in the 1980s, as anything but loathsome?' The film *Slumdog Millionaire* sees corrupt gangsters blind and maim street children to become beggars for their own financial gain.

We dare not call this a 'feast day', and the day of the Holy Innocents cuts through the inaccurate and domesticated pictures we keep of a Christ child born in a cosy stable we buy into each Christmas. For the reality is that Jesus was a refugee child too, born in dangerous conditions – at the back of a pub, in a cold outhouse and amid a rum collection of strange individuals and animals. No gas and air, no toast and tea after the birth, no warm hospital or vigilant nurse. Like hundreds of children on the planet today, Jesus was born into insecurity and at various stages in his life also knew he needed to trust God. All parents worry about their child's health in those early days after birth. A quick ride in the car to get home to a snug cot and warm room is what both of my children received. But not so for Mary and Joseph, and we can only imagine their additional anxiety as they were told that the megalomaniacal King Herod was seriously out to get their son. It is the stuff of nightmares, for all parents want their child to be safe.

Herod was the man appointed by the Romans to be the king of the Jews. Like many people obsessed with their own power, he had the tendency to become neurotic and to behave in ways which were despotic. He was reputed to have killed three of his own sons as well as his mother-in-law and his second wife, so for these unknown children there was no hope of survival. God communicates with Joseph in a dream, warning him not to return to Bethlehem just yet but to take a detour to Egypt, where there will be a genuine chance of safety. Perhaps this is a narrative device Matthew uses to fulfil the prophecy that God's Son was indeed 'called out of Egypt'. The text tells of Herod's fury at being outwitted, duped by the Magi who do not return to tell the king the whereabouts of the child who (apparently) threatens the reign of this earthly monarch. And so the order goes out – all male children under the age of two are to be searched out and eliminated. As readers, as mothers and fathers of children too, we can hear the agonized cries as verse 18 of Matthew

2 so unequivocally states, 'A voice was heard in Ramah, wailing and loud lamentation, Rachel weeping for her children; she refused to be consoled, because they are no more.' This again is to fulfil an Old Testament prophecy – this time from Jeremiah.

We do not know how long the family stayed in Egypt, where they lived or indeed how they survived. In this sense they became like millions of migrants and asylum seekers on the planet; in March 2017, the UN stated that the number of refugees who have fled Syria now exceeds five million, with millions more displaced internally, and this is just within one country alone.[2] And for so many people who leave their homeland, it only feels safe when the despot dies, and it is only when Herod is no more that Joseph and Mary believe it is safe to return to their own country.

As this account is only to be found in the Gospel according to Matthew several scholars have doubted its historical authenticity. The meaning of the story is clear – the intended elimination of God's Son in order to prevent the fulfilling of the new covenant. But clearly God is just not going to let this happen, and Matthew is extremely concerned to state that Jesus is the intended Jewish Messiah through the fulfilment of the Old Testament prophecies connected with Hosea and Jeremiah. Many scholars have made connections with the resonances found in this account with the story of Moses, too.

Whenever parents lose children there is agony. At the time of writing, we remember the 100th anniversary of the Battle of the Somme, where thousands of young men – some still teenagers – lost their lives. One of the reasons why we commemorate such events is to remember the pain of it and to recognize that such pain in this life can indeed never be wiped away. It is interesting that Rachel is mentioned, for here we have a name, the *name* of a real live flesh-and-blood woman, a mother. This name marks a counterbalance to the fact that we are not told any of the names of the children who are slaughtered. They are anonymous, as are so many innocent child victims caught up in secret atrocities around the world.

Sarah Bessey, in her book *Out of Sorts: Making peace with an evolving faith*, writes an extraordinary chapter on the nature of such untold pain and challenges us to reflect on what we should do with it. 'Obey the sadness,' she says: do not try to alleviate it with the lazy theology of suffering such as this being part of 'God's plan' or tragedy happening because somehow our own faith is not strong enough. A woman who has been pregnant eight times but has only four children, she can genuinely talk with authenticity about loss. Whether it is our own personal stories of loss or bigger more horrific ones like the Holy Innocents, she returns to the deeply biblical, perhaps unfashionable concept of lament, advocating that providing support and listening to those who grieve is really the only appropriate response to such pain. Reflecting on his best friend losing his young wife to cancer and leaving two young girls, she describes her husband flying out to Colorado to provide practical and emotional companionship.

> What do I say? There is nothing to say? Stop thinking there is something to say to make it go away. It won't go away. Abandon your answers. Avoid your clichés. Don't blame God. Learn to sit in the sadness. This is not the end.[3]

And it is because this is not the end that we have a day such as the Holy Innocents. It is because there are *still* women and men lamenting the death of their small ones, *still* people in emotional and spiritual pain, that we remember. We remember with absolute certainty that their names are written on God's heart of never-forgetfulness.

Prayer ideas

- Pray for migrants, refugees and asylum seekers everywhere.
- Pray for children and young people who live in daily fear of their lives.
- Pray for those mourning the loss of their children and young people.
- Pray for an end to 'reigns of terror' and the removal of all corrupt and cruel leadership.

John Wycliffe
A brave Bible

It's healthy to have a love–hate relationship with the established Church. There have been times in my own life as a Christian when I have railed against the Church's stance and dealings with particular issues. The Church of England's history has sometimes been dark and tumultuous, with stories of corruption and unholiness abounding. Its ponderous decision-making process is double-edged; a careful weighing up of issues of ethics and tradition often over several decades can be frustrating for many, akin to trying to turn around a container ship. Yet holding all parties together can be a model to the world in terms of generosity and prayerful conclusions.

As the year turns, the Church of England remembers one of its greatest and most passionate reformers, John Wycliffe. English scholar, theologian, biblical translator and church reformer, Wycliffe spent a lifetime being an irritant of the then Catholic Church. Born in Yorkshire in 1330 he spent much of his time in and around Oxford, eventually becoming a fellow of Merton College and Master of Balliol. He gained a BA in theology in 1369 and a PhD in 1372. When the ecclesial establishment could stand it no more he was eventually removed from his wardenship of Canterbury Hall, which only fired his life-long hatred for all things monastic.

Wycliffe's reputation was established primarily in two ways. He attacked the privileged status of the Church as institution, its clergy and monastic orders, whose power, status and wealth had become an insidious and damaging witness to the loving service of Christ. For Wycliffe, the luxury and pomp of some parishes and their ceremonious show had become abhorrent to him – a far cry from the poverty and compassion of God's kingdom – and many others also sympathized. Those who followed Wycliffe's cause were called Lollards, a popular and derogatory name for those without academic credentials and those who had been educated in English rather than Latin, if indeed they had been educated at all. By the mid-fifteenth century the term had become synonymous with an understanding of heresy.

But Wycliffe and his supporters had good cause to needle the Church of the time. Practices which were considered 'popish' were heavily criticized, for Wycliffe believed that the Bible contained everything a person needed for salvation. The veneration of the saints, requiem masses, the theology of transubstantiation were all considered twisted habits of an ecclesial body which had become distorted by the devil. Even worse were practices which sound antiquated and corrupt in their obscurity – annates (a system of tithing to amass wealth for those who held the most ecclesiastical power) and simony (payment to a cleric for the privilege of obtaining an ecclesiastical office). For Wycliffe, the Church had become not a sign of God's action and grace but rather a fat and self-satisfied tycoon who wore a cloak made from pomposity and power. He believed clergy should abandon their material property and return to a life of poverty, simplicity and discipline.

During the fourteenth century the Black Death raged and Wycliffe believed that this was a judgement on unworthy clergy, particularly because the mortality rate among clerics was high. In the later fourteenth century he felt the need to propagate his ideas more widely so he began to express them in easily distributable tracts as well as longer works. These spread his ideas more rapidly and through them he continued to attack what he understood as the corrupt practices of the Church. Wycliffe was often protected by the royal family, who supported his ideas until his dismissal of transubstantiation lost him royal protection.

During the last quarter of the century attacks on Wycliffe and his followers became more focused. In May of 1377 Pope Gregory himself sent five copies of a papal bull against Wycliffe to various powerful clerics, and Wycliffe was summoned before the Archbishop of Canterbury, William Courtenay. But Wycliffe persisted in his passion to reform the Church, writing his famous 33 conclusions.

The second reason we remember and honour Wycliffe today is through his translation, along with a team of others, of the Vulgate Bible into Middle English, a version completed in 1382 and known as 'Wycliffe's Bible'. He was an advocate of the translation of the Bible into the vernacular, believing that ordinary people should have the opportunity to read its words and wisdom for themselves. Perhaps the fact that the Bible had previously remained in the hands of the clergy, who could interpret it how they wished (and often untruthfully), was another thorn in the flesh of a man who saw so many problems in how the Church operated. Historically it remains difficult to define Wycliffe's part in this translation, but it is undeniable that the initiative was his and its success rested on his determination and vision. Approximately 150 manuscripts containing parts of the translation still exist today and there can be no doubt that his contribution in making the biblical text more accessible had far-reaching consequences for the Christian faith in the British Isles.

Every year in our parish the Year 6 students at our local church primary school are given a copy of the Bible as a leaving gift. The translation of this has changed over the eight years I have been here, the latest being a funky cartoon version of many of the most well-known stories. The children accept this gift graciously but I sometimes wonder how many copies will get lost or become forgotten, left unopened and dusty on a bookshelf which competes with the Xbox. We are spoilt today in a society where there is a multitude of different translations, so many of which include creatively presented Bible notes and attractively produced text. Power to buy and read is not the only dynamic in our hands: choice is as well. How many children will choose to pick up a Bible, or even buy one if they don't possess a copy? But the profusion of possibilities to engage with the text has also arrived, with Bible apps on phones and iPads literally at the tap of a finger – which has surely got to be good news.

This year in our own diocese we are promoting a project called YBible, an initiative which seeks to encourage ordinary people to engage with the biblical texts more than they have previously done, and in sustainable and creative ways. As part of this a small booklet has been produced where 52 people from around the diocese have sent in their own favourite Bible verse with a short explanation. The Bible is probably the most appreciated as well as the most misunderstood book in the history of the world. The inspired word of God, it is perhaps possible to argue just about anything from within its pages. Over the years as a Christian pilgrim as well as a priestly leader I have been both oppressed and encouraged by its words, and indeed through the interpretation of others. I have carried, too, often an abiding sense of inadequacy – that as a liberal catholic I cannot pluck random verses and passages out to use as examples for my own theological arguments quite as well as my other more evangelical brethren.

But of late I have also understood that not knowing every chapter and verse of Leviticus does not matter so much. Rather, what does is that we engage with its words in an enthusiastic as well as a prayerful way. The spiritual practices of St Ignatius, such as meditating on the text and *Lectio Divina*, allow the spirit of its words to transcend arguments about literal and contextual interpretations, and enable us to understand the faithful and universal themes in the Bible in a way which connects them with our own lives, with potentially life-changing consequences. And miraculous and encouraging stories of conversion are told the world over by surprising people who have interacted with the text, from the casual picking up of a Gideon Bible in a hotel when someone was at a low ebb to the hearing of simple verses in a vast cathedral.

One of my favourite places in the whole world is the small farm and estate of Ty Mawr in the tranquil Wybrnant Valley in North Wales. Here, Bishop William Morgan first translated the Bible into Welsh, a task commissioned by Elizabeth I and one which took him ten years to complete. The significance of this work is perhaps lost on many today, but the Welsh people had never previously been able to or allowed to worship in their own language. Henry VIII had ordered that only the English Bible be used in Wales, and before this only Latin ones were used. In Tudor Britain, the Bible was the only text ordinary people would have had access to and was the moral and spiritual backbone of society. Ty Mawr now welcomes visitors from all over the world who, inspired by the witness of this quiet place, leave as gifts copies of the Bible translated into numerous languages.

John Wycliffe's actions and theology were formally condemned in 1381. This was the year of the Peasants' Revolt, where itinerant preachers spread Wycliffe's ideas and beliefs like a forest fire. Wycliffe's witness is understood now as paving the way to the English Reformation, commemorated in its 500th anniversary in 2017. At the end of December 1384 Wycliffe suffered a stroke as he was saying Mass and he died as the year ended. In 1415 the Council of Constance declared Wycliffe a heretic and banned his writings. His body was even exhumed and burned and his ashes cast into the River Swift, which flowed through his parish of Lutterworth.

There can be no doubt that Wycliffe stands as a prophet of biblical proportions, with his witness to the power and purity of both Church and text. Some words from Wycliffe's *The Pastoral Office*:

It seems that the knowledge of God's law should be taught in that language which is best known, because this knowledge is God's Word. When Christ says in the gospel that both heaven and earth shall pass away but his words shall not pass away, he means by his 'words' his knowledge. Thus, God's knowledge is holy Scripture that may in no wise be false. Also, the Holy Spirit gave to the apostles at Pentecost knowledge to know all manner of languages to teach the peoples God's law thereby; and so, God willed that the people be taught his law in divers tongues. But what man on God's behalf should reverse God's ordinance and his will?[1]

Advent and Christmas are seasons where familiar texts are read and heard, appreciated and savoured, as well as taken for granted. The birth narratives of Jesus are well known even in our primarily non-Christian culture, together with the more mystical words at the beginning of the Gospel of John, listened to with awe and fascination. The Bible then is still, thankfully, deeply and immovably embedded into our culture – a living and Spirit-filled book, constantly ready to prove an agent of transformation to those who open and are open to it.

Prayer ideas

- Pray for the Gideons International and the Bible Society.
- Pray for biblical scholars and those who seek to teach and preach the faith.
- Pray for countries where it is a dangerous thing to own and read the Bible.
- Pray for there to be responsible reading and studying of the text within all church traditions.

Thomas Becket
Holy man, unholy death

———◆◆◆———

Unholy things take place in holy places. Alberta King, mother of Martin Luther King Jr, was shot and killed as she played the organ for the morning service in her church of Ebenezer Baptist in Atlanta, Georgia. In 1993 at the Anglican Church of St James, Kenilworth, South Africa, three members of the Azanian People's Liberation Army opened fire on members of the congregation.[1] Eleven people died and 58 were wounded. At the time the world felt the shock of relatively unheard of 'terrorist' attacks. In 1998 the attackers were granted amnesty through their participation in the Truth and Reconciliation Commission.

Thomas Becket, Archbishop of Canterbury in twelfth-century England, was violently pursued and killed, in the aisles of the most ancient church in the land, Canterbury Cathedral. Born in 1119, Becket became a senior cleric in an age of political turbulence and strife. He found himself in continual conflict with Henry II, believing that much of the Church and many of the clergy were becoming pampered and privileged. That Becket was a thorn in Henry's side is in no doubt and the most famously cited frustration from the king is, 'Who will rid me of this troublesome priest?' This demand, if not historically accurate, certainly conveys the difficult relationship between the two. The historian Simon Schama prefers the phrase from Becket's official biographer, Edward Grim, who offers a translation from the Latin: 'What miserable drones and traitors have I nourished and brought up in my household, who let their lord be treated with such shameful contempt by a low-born cleric?'[2]

In June 1170, the then Archbishop of York, along with the Bishops of London and Salisbury, crowned the heir apparent at York.[3] This was a breach of the power and decision-making of the Archbishop of Canterbury, and by November of the same year Becket had swiftly excommunicated all three clerics. The bishops fled to France, where the young king-to-be was residing, and with follow-up extractions from the established Church Henry decided to act. On 29 December 1170, four knight-representatives of the king arrived at Canterbury. The story goes that they hid their weapons outside and entered the cathedral in the hope of simply challenging the Archbishop. The knights told Becket that he had been summoned to Winchester to explain his recent actions, but he refused to go. It was at this point that the men retrieved their weapons and went back inside with the intent to kill him. Becket was preparing to say the service of Vespers but was mown down by these king's knights. Again, Edward Grim recounts the grisly tale of Becket being struck three times until he fell, defenceless, to the floor. The crown of Becket's head was reputedly sliced off, with blood and brains pouring on to the floor of this holy place. Becket's assassins fled north, finding sanctuary for a year at Knaresborough Castle, the residence of Hugh de Morville. For his part, Henry did not arrest these men or confiscate their lands, but nor did he help when they sought advice for their future the following year. Pope Alexander III eventually excommunicated all four men and they did penance by serving for several years in the Holy Land.

Soon after his death Becket began to be revered as a martyr throughout Europe, and on 21 February 1173 he was made a saint by the Pope. Later that year Becket's sister Mary was appointed Abbess of Barking Abbey as official reparation for the murder of her brother. Subsequently, Henry himself decided on a demonstration of public penance at Becket's tomb sometime during 1173 or 1174. The well-known play *Murder in the Cathedral* by T. S. Eliot describes the story of the assassination of Thomas and has kept the story alive for modern audiences. First performed in 1935, the play draws on Grim's eye-witness biography and its theme of standing up against unjust authority, which paralleled advancing fascism in Europe.

Nowadays a powerful metal sculpture created by the architect Giles Blomfield marks the spot of Becket's martyrdom at Canterbury. It hangs above the Becket altar and consists of a large cross set alongside two elongated swords with red at their tips. Spotlit, the swords produce two further swords in shadow, thus symbolizing the four knights who killed the Archbishop.

For me, the fact that this piece of art was designed by Blomfield is an interesting connection with my own life and my own experience of the double-edged nature of official 'holy' places. Blomfield originated in Truro, the city where I grew up. My father's final post was as Canon Chancellor at Truro Cathedral and my childhood experience was one where the carefree nature of adolescence was offset with the tensions and toxicity that cathedral ministry often brings. Clergy can be self-important and pompous; mission doesn't happen. In my case my mother left, deciding to worship in a more ordinary and sincere parish. Yet it was crouched in the stalls participating in Book of Common Prayer Evensong (still not a desperately child-friendly service) that I believe the first whispers of calling emerged in my heart. It was here that I experienced the magic of a majestic Christingle service, a packed cathedral of whispering and awe-struck children standing in candlelit and hallowed gloom; here that I first gained a sense of the power and diversity of a community of Christian people trying, failing, but persevering in their following of Jesus.

Unholy things happen in places which are supposed to be holy but the opposite is also true. Holy things, God-things, happen in places which often have dubious or at least agnostic reputations. In my own parish, we have a women's prison. Recently members of the local churches and general community were invited to hear a small group of women publicly explain their actions and apologize for their crimes.[4] Most of those from my parish were in tears as a result of this restorative justice programme: the honesty, sincerity and vulnerability they heard from the women was something which was truly admired by those listening. In groups afterwards support and recognition were offered to those brave enough to 'go public'.

I heard a retired bishop once tell the story of a fresh expression of church planned in a local pub. The bishop was drawn in to be 'the main attraction' on one of the evenings. He agreed, on the proviso that everyone choosing to attend brought someone who was unused to church and who perhaps only had a tentative interest in the faith. When he arrived, the pub was packed, but to the bishop's dismay he realized that everyone within sight was already a believer. The dejected barman selling a multiplicity of soft drinks pointed him to a room around the back. The bishop disappeared and discovered a small collection of regulars holding real drinks. As he approached the group, one woman, seeing the purple, said to him, 'I'm not a bad person, life has just treated me harshly.' The bishop, looking at her in compassion, took off his pectoral cross and put it round her neck, in affirmation of life's bruising. This is a story which speaks of holiness in an unexpected place. A broken woman, seeing a tall cleric symbolizing the judgement of the Church, offered her own experience of a life of pain and recrimination but was perhaps taken aback by an unexpected encounter of kindness and healing.[5]

The story of Christmas also has unexpected grace happening in the surprising domain of a back room. Stables are not usually associated with holiness or sanctuary and yet it was here amid steaming and stinking beasts that the Son of God was introduced to the world. This season we will have many people who will enter our churches for not very worthy reasons – to watch their children play starring roles in the Nativity, because the pubs have closed or because they are staying with the relatives and must fit in with their churchgoing parents-in-law. There will be many too who will also behave in not very holy ways in buildings we hold dear – there will be gum-chewing, crisp-crunching, people will whisper all through the service and a mobile will inevitably go off, ruining the ambience. But through it all, if we let it, holiness will descend. It will descend because, within that two-second stillness, that reverent hush (even if it is for all the wrong reasons as the play begins to start), we will experience that warm feeling which tells us we are so happy to be with those we really love, as we feel the presence of the Christ child, tangibly with us, *Emmanuel*. Advent is the big story of lots of small stories of God working through unworthiness, through unexpected people, places and situations; it is the story of holiness flowing through surprise, watering the ground of what could have been an ugly back yard, to grow the seeds of a future blossoming with divine hope.

Prayer ideas

- Pray for all who work in cathedral ministry.
- Pray for those who feel a vocation to challenge injustice and inequality, especially in the Church.
- Pray for those who do holy things in ordinary places.
- Pray for all who will lead worship during Advent and at Christmas in Christian as well as spiritually inquisitive places.

Notes

Advent saints

Andrew: a life less ordinary

1 Dietrich Bonhoeffer, 'The cost of discipleship', in Robert Atwell (ed.), *Celebrating the Saints: Daily spiritual readings*, Norwich: Canterbury Press, 1988, p. 452.
2 Bonhoeffer, 'The cost of discipleship', p. 452.
3 Richard Chartres, 'Listen to the Spirit – on the bus', *Church Times*, 12 February 2016.
4 Chartres, 'Listen to the Spirit'.
5 Bonhoeffer, 'The cost of discipleship', p. 452.

Charles de Foucauld: with and not for

1 John V. Taylor, *The Go-Between God*, London: SCM Press, 1973, p. 228.
2 From <www.hermitary.com/articles/foucauld.html 2010>.
3 Mark Gibbard, 'Charles de Foucauld', in Cheslyn Jones, Geoffrey Wainwright and Edward Yarnold (eds), *The Study of Spirituality*, London: SPCK, 1986, p. 421.
4 From <www.hermitary.com/articles/foucauld.html 2010>.
5 *Rev*, Series 3: Episode 1, Big Talk Productions, 2014.

Francis Xavier: pioneer of the East

1 Robert Atwell (ed.), *Celebrating the Saints: Daily spiritual readings*, Norwich: Canterbury Press, 1988, p. 502.
2 Hannah Ward and Jennifer Wild (compilers), *The Lion Christian Quotation Collection*, Oxford: Lion, 1997, p. 109.
3 Nadia Bolz-Weber, *Accidental Saints: Finding God in all the wrong people*, Norwich: Canterbury Press, 2015, pp. 47 and 48.

John of Damascus: matter matters

1 From John of Damascus, *On the Incarnation and the Holy Icons*, quoted in Robert Atwell, *Celebrating the Saints: Daily spiritual readings*, Norwich: Canterbury Press, 1988, p. 459.
2 Atwell, *Celebrating the Saints*, p. 459.

Nicholas Ferrar: new monastic

1 From a conversation between the poet Malcolm Guite and Lancia E. Smith; see <lanciaesmith.com/waiting-on-the-word-for-advent/>, 11 November 2015.
2 See <lanciaesmith.com/waiting-on-the-word-for-advent>.
3 *Common Worship: Pastoral Services* (London: Church House Publishing, 2005), p. 105. Reproduced by permission.
4 Shane Claiborne, *The Irresistible Revolution*, Grand Rapids, Michigan: Zondervan, 2006, p. 201.

Nicholas: bearer of gifts

1 Hannah Ward and Jennifer Wild (compilers), *The Lion Christian Quotation Collection*, Oxford: Lion, 1997, p. 286.
2 See 'Real stories of meaningful Christmas gifts' at <www.familylife.com/articles/topics/holidays/featured/christmas/real-stories-of-meaningful-christmas-gifts>.

Ambrose: when in Rome, do as the Romans do

1 A heresy denying the divinity of Christ, Arianism was formulated by the Alexandrian priest Arius, who lived between about 250 and 336. It maintains that the Son of God was created by God the Father, which clashes with an understanding of a coequal and eternal Trinitarian God.
2 Hannah Ward and Jennifer Wild (compilers), *The Lion Christian Quotation Collection*, Oxford: Lion, 1997, p. 19.
3 Ward and Wild, *The Lion Christian Quotation Collection*, p. 19.

Lucy: new eyes

1 Douglas Rhymes, *Prayer in the Secular City*, Cambridge: Lutterworth Press, 1967, p. 68, as quoted in Hannah Ward and Jennifer Wild (compilers), *The Lion Christian Meditation Collection*, Oxford: Lion, 1998, p. 283.
2 Ruth Burrows, *Ascent to Love*, ed. Elizabeth Ruth Obbard, London: Darton, Longman and Todd, 1988, p. 48, as quoted in Ward and Wild, *The Lion Christian Meditation Collection*, p. 188.
3 Clement of Alexandria, *An Exhortation to the Greeks*, as quoted in Robert Atwell, *Celebrating the Saints: Daily spiritual readings*, Norwich: Canterbury Press, 1988, p. 469.

Samuel Johnson: moral messaging

1 Jack Lynch, *Samuel Johnson's Dictionary*, New York: Walker Books, 2003, p. 2.
2 Walter Jackson Bate, *Samuel Johnson*, New York: Harcourt Brace

Jovanovich, 1997, p. 281, quoted in <en.wikipedia.org/wiki/The_Vanity_of_Human_Wishes>.

3 Donald Greene, *Samuel Johnson: Updated Edition*, Boston: Twayne Publishers, 1989, p. 87, quoted in <en.wikipedia.org/wiki/Samuel_Johnson>.

4 Howard Weinbrot, *Aspects of Samuel Johnson: Essays on his arts, mind, afterlife and politics*, Newark, New Jersey: University of Delaware, 2005, p. 105.

5 From Micah Purnell, 'Rising', *Segment Magazine*, 1; see <www.segmentmag.com> Issue 1.

John of the Cross: our deepest yearning

1 'Discalced' means 'unshod'. Teresa's reformed communities were so described because Carmelites tended to wear sandals rather than shoes. Discussed in Helen Marshall, *Total Cost and Total Transformation: Learning from St John of the Cross*, Cambridge: Grove, 2011.

2 Quoted in Marshall, *Total Cost*, p. 9. The translation is by Marjorie Flower OCD, *The Poems of St John of the Cross*, reproduced by kind permission of Varroville Carmel, Australia.

3 Quoted in Marshall, *Total Cost*, p. 9.

4 Rowan Williams, *The Wound of Knowledge: Christian spirituality from the New Testament to St John of the Cross*, London: Darton, Longman and Todd, 1979, p. 164.

5 Williams, *The Wound of Knowledge*.

6 E. Allison Peers, *Spirit of Flame: A study of St John of the Cross*, London: SCM Press, 1943, p. 118, quoted in Marshall, *Total Cost*, p. 6.

Eglantyne Jebb: Save the Children

1 From Richard Symonds, *Far Above Rubies: The women uncommemorated by the Church of England*, Leominster: Gracewing, 1993, quoted in Robert Atwell, *Celebrating the Saints: Daily spiritual readings*, Norwich: Canterbury Press, 1988, p. 476.

2 Jemima Thackray, 'Faith builds a future', *Church Times*, 8 April 2016, p. 24; also see the Faith Foundation website, <www.faithfoundation.rw/index-1.html>.

3 Hannah Ward and Jennifer Wild (compilers), *The Lion Christian Meditation Collection*, Oxford: Lion, 1998, p. 280.

Christmas saints

John the Baptist: unlikely prophet

1 Jim Yardley, 'Debating a change of faith under brutal captivity', *New York Times*, 21 February 2015.

2 Yardley, 'Debating a change of faith'.

3 Thomas Kelly, in Hannah Ward and Jennifer Wild (compilers), *The Lion Christian Quotation Collection*, Oxford: Lion, 1997, p. 212.

4 Antoinette Doolittle, in Ward and Wild, *The Lion Christian Quotation Collection*, p. 170.

Elizabeth: defying expectations

1 Hannah Ward and Jennifer Wild (compilers), *The Lion Christian Meditation Collection*, Oxford: Lion, 1998, p. 322.

2 Hannah Ward and Jennifer Wild (compilers), *The Lion Christian Quotation Collection*, Oxford: Lion, 1997, p. 285.

Zechariah: mute and miracle

1 Marilynne Robinson, *Lila*, London: Virago, 2014, p. 19.

Joseph: anti-abandonment

1 Quoted in Will Gompertz, *Think Like an Artist*, London: Penguin, 2015, p. 36.

2 Hannah Ward and Jennifer Wild (compilers), *The Lion Christian Quotation Collection*, Oxford, Lion, 1997, p. 205.

The Wise Men: recognizing God

1 Andrew Davison (ed.), *Amazing Love: Theology for understanding discipleship, sexuality and mission*, London: Darton, Longman and Todd, 2016.

2 Patrick Hart and Jonathan Montaldo (eds), *The Intimate Merton: His life from his journals* Oxford: Lion, 1990, p. 70.

3 Hannah Ward and Jennifer Wild (compilers), *The Lion Christian Meditation Collection*, Oxford: Lion, 1998, p. 282.

Saintly shepherds: sacred staying

1 James Rebanks, *The Shepherd's Life*, London: Allen Lane/Penguin, 2015, p. 73.

2 Rebanks, *Shepherd's Life*, p. 88.

3 Rebanks, *Shepherd's Life*, p. 285.

4 Barbara Brown Taylor, *Mixed Blessings: Being the people of God*, Norwich: Canterbury Press, 1998, p. 49.

Stephen: we are connected

1 Robert Atwell, *Celebrating the Saints: Daily spiritual readings*, Norwich: Canterbury Press, 1988, p. 477.

2 '*Railway Man* true story vs movie – real Eric Lomax, Takashi Nagase', at <www.historyvshollywood.com/reelfaces/railway-man/>.

3 Mary Grey, *The Wisdom of Fools: Seeking revelation for today*, London: SPCK, 1993, p. 67.

John the Apostle and Evangelist: I am with you

1 From Oscar Romero, *The Church is All of You: Thoughts of Archbishop Oscar Romero*, comp. and trans. James R. Brockman SJ, New York: Winston Press, 1984, p. 75, as quoted in Hannah Ward and Jennifer Wild (compilers), *The Lion Christian Meditation Collection*, Oxford: Lion, 1998, p. 187.

2 Barbara Brown Taylor, *Mixed Blessings; Being the people of God*, Norwich: Canterbury Press, p. 36.

Holy Innocents: lives never forgotten

1 Jim Thompson, *Stepney Calling: Thoughts for our day*, Oxford: Mowbray, 1991, as quoted in Hannah Ward and Jennifer Wild (compilers), *The Lion Christian Meditation Collection*, Oxford: Lion, 1998, p. 60.

2 From <www.aljazeera.com>, 17 March 2017.

3 Sarah Bessey, *Out of Sorts: Making peace with an evolving faith*, London: Darton, Longman and Todd, 2015, pp. 191–2.

John Wycliffe: a brave Bible

1 Robert Atwell, *Celebrating the Saints: Daily spiritual readings*, Norwich: Canterbury Press, 1988, p. 487.

Thomas Becket: holy man, unholy death

1 At the time, the APLA was the military wing of the Pan Africanist Congress, a nationalist movement in South Africa which disbanded in 1994.

2 Simon Schama, *History of Britain; Volume 1*, London: BBC Books, 2000, p. 142.

3 This was something of a common practice during the Middle Ages. The heirs of existing monarchs were often crowned when still children or young people to avoid any controversy and dispute in terms of succession. The practice began in France but later moved to England and other places in Europe. However, these 'junior kings' had diminished power.

4 Supporting Offenders through Restoration Inside, or SORI, is part of a programme of restorative justice.

5 I am grateful for this beautiful story, told at an event I co-led with Bishop Cyril Ashton for Liverpool Diocese in 2016.